CONTEMPLATION
IN ACTION

CONTEMPLATION IN ACTION

RICHARD ROHR
AND FRIENDS

A Crossroad Book
The Crossroad Publishing Company
New York

The essays in this volume were all previously published in *Radical Grace,* the quarterly publication of the Center for Action and Contemplation (CAC) in Albuquerque, New Mexico. *Radical Grace* includes the most recent work of the founder of the CAC, Fr. Richard Rohr, along with up-to-date information on the CAC's conferences, internships, and available resources. For more information go to *www.cacradicalgrace.org.*

The Crossroad Publishing Company
www.CrossroadPublishing.com

"The Duty of Confrontation" by Thomas Keating first appeared as a chapter in *Awakenings,* published by The Crossroad Publishing Company, 1992.

Printed in the United States of America

The text of this book is set in 11/15 Galliard.
The display fonts are Kaufmann, Cochin, and Univers.

Library of Congress Cataloging-in-Publication Data

Rohr, Richard.
   Contemplation in action / Richard Rohr and friends.
   p. cm.
   ISBN 0-8245-2388-1 (alk. paper)
   1. Contemplation. 2. Christian life. I. Title.
   BV5091.C7R635 2006
   242 – dc22

                     2006003938

ISBN-10: 0-8245-2388-1
ISBN-13: 978-0-8245-2388-6

    5   6   7   8   9   10   12   11   10

Contents

Part Two
TO LOVE TENDERLY

Part Three
TO WALK HUMBLY WITH YOUR GOD

Center for
Action and Contemplation

Our Mission

The Center for Action and Contemplation

Supports a new reformation

From the inside!

~ In the spirit of the Gospels

~ Confirming people's deeper spiritual intuitions

~ Encouraging actions of justice rooted in prayer

~ With a new appreciation for, and cooperation with, other denominations, religions, and cultures

Our Core Principles

- The teaching of Jesus is our central reference point.
  (*criterion*)

- We need a contemplative mind in order to do compassionate action.
  (*process*)

- The best criticism of the bad is the practice of the better. Oppositional energy only creates more of the same.
  (*emphasis*)

- Practical truth is more likely found at the bottom and the edges than at the top or the center of most groups, institutions, and cultures.
  (*perspective*)

- We will support true authority, the ability to "author" life in others, regardless of the group.
  (*non tribal*)

- Life is about discovering the right questions more than having the right answers.
  (*primacy of discernment*)

- True religion leads us to an experience of our True Self and undermines my false self.
  (*ultimate direction*)

This is what Yahweh asks of you; only this:
to act justly,
to love tenderly,
and to walk humbly with your God.

— Micah 6:8

A Publisher's Welcome

The Crossroad Publishing Company welcomes you to *Contemplation in Action*. If you've visited the Center for Action and Contemplation in Albuquerque, New Mexico, you already know how the Center nourishes spiritual seekers. Perhaps you knew Richard Rohr from his cassettes and books, and came to hear lectures by him and other guest speakers. Perhaps you came to volunteer for a season, or to learn more about the Men as Learners and Elders (MALE) movement. Or perhaps, like many, you've never personally visited the Center but have always supported its mission and have learned much about it in the *Radical Grace* newsletter.

Whatever your connection to the Center, this book will help introduce you to many of the voices who've contributed to the Center's life. As you read through the book, we encourage you to apply the ideas, questions, and reflection to your own life — are you being called to new ways of contemplation and action? We also encourage you to act. If you can't make the trip to New Mexico, to sit in the desert sun with the colorful Sandia mountains rising in the distance and a labyrinth marking your path, your best destination is the Center's website at *www.cacradicalgrace.org*.

See you there!

The Publisher

Part One

TO ACT JUSTLY

1

Contemplation and Compassion
The Second Gaze

RICHARD ROHR, O.F.M.

Contemplation happens to everyone. It happens in moments when we are open, undefended, and immediately present.
— Dr. Gerald May

 My immediate response to most situations is with reactions of attachment, defensiveness, judgment, control, and analysis. I am better at calculating than contemplating. Let's admit that we all start there. The false self seems to have the "first gaze" at almost everything.

On my better days, when I am "open, undefended, and immediately present," I can sometimes begin with a contemplative mind and heart. Often I can *get* there later and even *end* there, but it is usually a second gaze. The True Self seems to always be ridden and blinded by the defensive needs of the false self. It is an hour-by-hour battle, at least for me. I can see why all spiritual traditions insist on daily prayer, in fact, morning, midday, evening, and before-we-go-to-bed prayer too! Otherwise, I can assume that I am back in the cruise control of small and personal self-interest, the pitiable and fragile "richard" self.

The first gaze is seldom compassionate. It is too busy weighing and feeling itself: "How will this affect me?" or "How does my self-image demand that I react to this?" or "How can I get back in control of this situation?" This leads us to an implosion, a self preoccupation that cannot enter into communion with the other or the moment. In other words, we first feel *our* feelings before we can relate to the situation and emotion of the *other.* Only after God has taught us how to live "undefended" can we immediately stand with and for the other, and for the moment. It takes lots of practice. Maybe that is why many people even speak of their "spiritual practice"?

My practice is probably somewhat unique because of the nature of my life. I have no wife, family, or even constant community. My Franciscan tradition and superiors have allowed me in these later years to live alone, in a little "hermitage" behind the friary and parish, that I call East of Eden. I am able to protect long hours of silence and solitude each day (when I am home), which I fill with specific times of prayer, study, journaling and writing, spiritual reading, gardening, walking, and just gazing. It is a luxury that most of you do not have. (My 50 percent of time on the road is much harder to balance, and probably more like your life.)

On a practical level, my at-home day is two extremes: both very busy (visitors and calls, counselees, work at the

CAC, mail, writing, and some work at Holy Family parish), yet on the opposite side my life is very quiet and alone. I avoid most social gatherings, frankly because I know *my soul has other questions to ask and answer as I get older* (thank God, my Franciscan community has honored this need). Small talk and "busyness about many things" will not get me there. If I am going to continue to address groups, as if I have something to say, then I have to really know what I know, really believe what I believe, and my life has to be more experiential and intimate than mere repetition of formulas and doctrines. I am waiting, practicing, and asking for the second gaze.

I suppose this *protected interiority* was the historic meaning of cloister, vows of silence, silence in church, and guarded places and times inside of monasteries, where you were relieved of all the usual social pleasantries and obligations. Some had to be free to move beyond ego consciousness to deeper contact with the unconscious, the shadow self, the intimate journey of the soul, toward conscious union with God. Traditionally, you were never allowed to live as a "hermit" until later in life, and only after you had paid your dues to community and concrete relationships. Only community and marriage force you to face, own, and exorcise your own demons. Otherwise, loners are just misanthropes or sociopaths, people with poor social skills, or people who desire to have total control of their day and time. This is not holiness. Avoiding people does not compute into love of God; being quiet and alone does not make you into a contemplative. Introversion and shyness are not the same as inner peace or communion.

"Still waters run deep," they say, but that water can be either very clear or quite toxic.

Your practice must somehow include the problem. Prayer is not the avoiding of distractions, but precisely how you deal with distractions. Contemplation is not the avoidance of the problem, but a daily merging with the problem, and finding its full resolution. What you quickly and humbly learn in contemplation, is that *how you do anything is probably how you do everything*. If you are brutal in your inner reaction to your own littleness and sinfulness, your social relationships and even your politics will probably be the same — brutal. One sees a woman overcome this split in an autobiography like St. Therese of Lisieux's *Story of a Soul*. This young contemplative nun is daily dealing with her irritations, judgments, and desire to run from her fellow sisters in the convent. She faces her own mixed motives and pettiness. She is constant in her concern for those working actively in the missions. But her goal is always compassion and communion. She suffers her powerlessness until she can finally break through to love. *She holds the tension within herself (the essence of contemplation) until she herself is the positive resolution of that tension.* Therese always gets to the second gaze.

It has taken me much of my life to begin to get to the second gaze. By nature I have a critical mind and a demanding heart, and I am impatient. These are both my gifts and my curses, as you might expect. Yet I cannot have one without the other, it seems. I cannot risk losing touch with either my angels or my demons. They are both good teachers. A life of solitude and silence allows them both, and invariably leads me to the second gaze. The gaze of compassion, looking out at life from the place of Divine Intimacy is really all I have, and all I have to give, even though I don't always do it.

I named my little hermitage "East of Eden" for some very specific reasons, not, however, because of John Steinbeck's marvelous novel (and movie) of the same name. On a humorous level, it was because I moved here six years ago, there hundred yards "east" of Holy Family Friary where I had previously lived. We had a fine community while I was there, consisting of three priests, two brothers, and many visitors who genuinely enjoyed one another — most of the time anyway! All my needs and desires were met in very good ways. It was a sort of "Eden."

But I also picked the name because of its significance in the life of Cain, after he had killed his brother Abel. It was a place where God sent Cain, this bad boy, after he had failed and sinned, yet ironically with a loving and protective mark: "So Yahweh put a mark on Cain so that no one would do him harm. He sent him to wander in the land of Nod, east of Eden" (Genesis 4:16).

By my late fifties I had had plenty of opportunities to see my own failures, shadow, and sin. The first gaze at myself was critical, negative, and demanding, not helpful at all, to me or to others. I am convinced that such guilt and shame are never from God. They are merely the protestations of the false self as it is shocked at its own poverty — the defenses of a little man who wants to be big man. God leads by compassion toward the soul, never by condemnation. If God would relate to us by severity and punitiveness, God would only be giving us permission to do the same (which is tragically, exactly what has happened!). God offers us, instead, the grace to "weep" over our sins more than to ever perfectly overcome them, to humbly recognize our littleness rather than become big. It is the way of Cain, Francis, and Therese. It is a kind of weeping and a kind of wandering that keeps us both askew and awake.

So now my later life call is to "wander in the land of Nod," enjoying God's so often proven love and protection, and look back at my life, and everybody's life, the One-And-Only-Life, marked happily and gratefully with the sign of Cain. Contemplation and compassion are finally coming together. This is my second gaze. It is well worth waiting for, because only the second gaze sees fully and truthfully. It sees itself, the other, and even God with God's own eyes, which are always eyes of compassion.

2

Playing the Prophet Close

RICHARD ROHR, O.F.M.

In the church, God has given the first place to apostles, the second to prophets, the third to teachers. (1 Cor. 12:28)

In this time, when the United States seems to be setting itself up for a perpetual war posture, when the Pentagon can get by with trillions of dollars of unaccountable funds, when a kind of unthinking patriotism seems to be the ideal, it is going to be all the more important that prophetic voices be clear, grounded, and very certain trumpets. Here at the Center for Action and Contemplation, we try to call forth the prophetic charism in what we call the "third way." It is different from direct advocacy of a certain political or theological opinion. It is also different from denying the problem or looking the other way. It is waiting and thinking and praying until something more refined emerges, until God has had a chance to speak, and until we have truly heard the other position. The third way is neither fight nor flight. It is, as someone wisely put it, "holding the opposites together long enough till you know they are not true." Another word for it is contemplation.

21

Since most of our readers are of a more progressive mind-set, this essay will first amount to a "third way critique" of the so-called liberal response, so that the peace movement can bring true and holy liberation to the issues at hand. American liberalism does not tend to build anything that lasts. This new imperialism in America is too self-assured and too disguised to be resolved with any flash-in-the-pan kinds of fires. We need a more purified and enduring fire now, which means we need some real prophets. A prophet must first of all be capable of spiritual depth — and that always includes *a demanding capacity for self-criticism and honesty.* We must first of all play the prophet to ourselves before we can dare to be prophetic for America or for the churches. Those are the only prophets worth trusting, and right now, neither knee-jerk pacifism nor knee-jerk patriotism seems to be guided by the Spirit. Finally, a prophet must be able to challenge both ends of the spectrum, but he or she has to start at home base.

Prophecy for the Liberals

"Liberal" is a term that became a household word in America only in the 1960s. Before that time, we were all just Americans, middle class, and Judeo-Christian. After the postmodern mind emerged in the late 1960s, we have taken sides on just about everything. We disagree about what the very goal of life is, and we surely disagree on how to get there. The postmodern mind rejects in principle any "big story." There is only the individual, and the social constructs that we create.

I fear that the conservatives will have their endless war against terrorism because the liberals are incapable of doing anything together — beyond analysis and protest itself. Liberals seem unable to call their own consumer lifestyles into question. They cannot see their complicity in the system and thus cannot radically critique it. You cannot make an art form out of critique itself; it is not the kind of deep passion or positive faith that can stand up to war, or vengeance, or long-haul injustice. It hooks the negative voices inside of all of us, which the young especially do not yet need. They have not yet found a truly positive vision. You have to be able to find a deep yes before you can dare to say no.

Let's try to explain how we got to this strange point. What were the two underlying worldviews that made us divide so sharply in the 1960s, and from which we have still not recovered? The dominant worldview was what we now call a traditional worldview. It was based on supposedly religious values of loyalty, hard work, obedience, law and order, and a clear sense of a transcendent goal of "heaven." Not too much concern about justice or truth *here,* but it did perform a strong social function. We could get justice and truth later, but our job was to make the best of this world by love of family, religion, and personal sacrifice. It worked in many ways and gave a lot of people superficially happy lives both at the top and at the bottom of the pile. We at least knew where we stood in the great scheme of things, and that took away a huge amount of anger and anxiety. But this worldview was built on massive and denied injustice and oppression. We were blissfully unaware of the dark side of our successes, our money, our wars, our racism, our sexism, and our "self-evident truths."

So the opposite had to show itself. By 1968 the tidal wave had landed full force in America. "How could we have been so blind? How could we have not seen what was hidden in plain sight?" Thirty years later we are still living in guilt, shame, and a pendulum swing of reaction to our stupidity about injustice. "We are never going to be so wrong again! In fact, we will find a way to be perfectly right!" It is called American liberalism, and it is half right; it has initiated many crucial social reforms. But it is also half wrong, and is largely incapable of seeing this.

The brilliant Huston Smith puts it this way: "The goals it [postmodernism] espouses are mainly the right ones, but *the question is whether the climate of opinion it builds is conducive to the realization of those very goals* [emphasis added]." If you want strong social cohesion, compelling vision, or in-depth transformation, you almost always have to resort to very traditional groups and values! This is very humiliating to admit for liberal types. Only the Dorothy Days can go to the local parish Mass on Sunday and critique the cardinal and mayor of New York on Monday. The connection between tradition and critique is at the heart of the prophetic charism. The Hebrew prophets were always radical traditionalists. By their definition, most liberals are not radical *enough,* and most conservatives are not traditional at all.

In my experience, *liberalism creates suspicious people more than loving people.* They begin by asking, "Who has the power here?" instead of, "How can I serve here?" Life is an issue to be informed about or fixed, but seldom a mystery to participate in — even in its broken state. That is probably the core difference between a mere liberal and a truly transformed individual.

Liberals need to find that rare ability to live happily in a broken world, and still work for its reform. It is a work of art that I believe only spirituality can achieve. Mere ideology is not sufficient to the task. Behind every cynic I meet, there was once a youthful idealist who could not make his ideas work outside of his head. Liberals seem incapable of being a part of a tainted anything: food, institutions, histories, explanations, groups, churches, and most especially authority structures of any kind. Soon they themselves cannot lead — or follow good leaders, because they mistrust power and leadership itself. Yet, history makes it clear that good leadership is necessary for real change.

American liberalism, in my opinion, has no practical goal beyond maintaining personal and social freedom. "I choose, therefore I am" might be its operational belief system. The problem for the peace movement is that you cannot build any new social structures or enduring constituencies within this belief system. Such movements deconstruct from within, as the highly opinionated individualists quickly come into conflict with one another's freedom to think. What they lack is a spiritual center, a Reference Point outside of the private "I."

We religious folks would say they lack God, especially a God who gives source, pattern, and external goal. As a result, we each become our own source, pattern, and goal. The First Commandment was not accidentally the first, because if you don't have "one God before you," you will always become your own god. For this reason it is difficult to build anything cohesive or compelling among liberal people. There is no authority beyond individual opinion and recent research, and in fact, the very word "authority" is considered bad. Compare that to the true "liberalism" of a Martin Luther King, or a Dorothy Day, or a Cesar Chavez. They all had an authority beyond their own — and a Center outside of themselves.

Prophecy for the Conservatives

If liberals refuse to be a part of the dirt of history, conservatives refuse to even see the dirt — at least in their own group! They hunker down and call their evil "good." The conservative response is usually the common person's first response to reality: "What is in place already should probably be trusted. It must be true, because that is the way it is." Its basic sin is lack of courage, but also lack of exposure or education. It usually does not "know" about the dark side, the other side, the view from the bottom, or even the view from the top. Sometimes it is innocence, often a false innocence engendered by fear, but always a costly innocence for somebody — maybe even for themselves. It confuses loyalty to systems with loyalty to God. We Americans call it a "redneck" response, pointing to its uneducated origins, but actually many rich and educated people are conservative for their own political and economic purposes. The first group I call "value conservatives"; the second I call "power conservatives." Usually the value conservatives can grow and change. It is the power conservatives who are usually trapped inside of self-interest.

Conservatives, in general, are so enamored with presidents and popes and precedents that there is never any room for prophecy or honest self-criticism. Do you ever hear George Will criticize the Republicans, or Mother Angelica criticize the Vatican? Their truth is often too small and too self-serving. Almost always "separatists" in some sense, they are usually on the run from some painful or unworthy place in themselves.

It seems to me that conservatives are enamored with past evils which they too easily call "good," whereas liberals are enamored with clever new evils which they think will destroy evil once and for all. Neither of them is willing to carry the burden of living tentatively in a passing and imperfect world. So the contemporary choice offered most Americans is *between unstable correctness (liberals) and stable illusion (conservatives)*! What a choice! We see this in the present war against terrorism, although those who want stable illusion seem to be in the great majority. It has little to do with real transformation in either case. How different from the radical traditionalism of a T. S. Eliot:

> You are not here to verify, instruct yourself, or inform curiosity or carry report. You are here to kneel....
>
> (*Little Gidding*)

The Third Way

There *is* a third way, and it probably is a way of "kneeling." Most people would just call it "wisdom," which is always distinguished from mere intelligence. It demands a transformation of consciousness and a move beyond the dualistic win/lose mind. Religion has always said that an authentic God encounter is the quickest and truest path to such wisdom. It is the *ultimate securing* that allows us to creatively deal with the essential impermanence and insecurity of everything else. It is the ultimate changing of Reference Point that puts self and everything else in proper perspective. No wonder it was called "conversion." The slow but steady path of contemplative practice can lead us here, as also does suffering and failure, which is probably the most common path.

We come to the third way only over time. In the words of W. H. Auden, "The garden is the only place there is, but you will not find it until you have looked for it everywhere and found nowhere that is not a desert" (*For the Time Being*). The Gospel accepts this essentially tragic nature of human existence; it is willing to bear the contradictions that are imprinted on all of reality. It will always be a road less traveled. Let's call it "unstable stability"! But for some reason, it is the only *real* stability, because it is a truthful map of reality, and it is always the truth that sets us free. It is contact with Reality that finally heals us. And contemplation, quite simply, is meeting reality in its most simple, immediate, and contradictory form. It is the resolving of those immense contradictions that characterizes the mystics, the saints, the prophets, and all those who pray. The result is always a "third something."

Those who can hold the paradox (both passionate belief *in* and then critical evaluation *of*), those who can live on the horns of this constant conservative/liberal dilemma, will build good things, and things that will last. They will represent that "universal catholicism" with which St. Augustine overcame the righteous Donatists of his day. Augustine said that we must throw out the net which gathers "fish of every kind," leaving all expelling and excluding to "the end of the age, when angels will separate" the chaff from the grain and the weeds from the wheat (Matt. 13:24–50). Neither expelling and excluding (conservative temptation), nor perfect explaining (liberal temptation) is our task. Frankly, we must hold Mother Angelica and Daniel Berrigan together in one embrace, which interestingly enough, she cannot do, but he can. We must hold nonviolent activists together with Islamic fundamentalists, even though fundamentalism cannot do the same. From that place alone we can discern who holds the true net of God, the net that includes and does not need to expel. In such a net you can allow *yourself* to be caught, and caught happily, because there will be room for you and for the other — and for divine mercy besides. Any other net is only a trap and a prison.

I would like to conclude with a stunning quote from my favorite Catholic theologian of the last century, Karl Rahner. I used to pray at his tomb when I was teaching in Innsbruck and often asked for his wisdom. Perhaps we can let Rahner help us to hold the paradox of (conservative) tradition and (liberal) critique *together* until we find a third graced way.

> I have had to accept the fact that my life is almost totally paradoxical. I have also had to learn gradually to get along without apologizing for that fact, even to myself. It is in the paradox itself, the paradox which was and still is a source of insecurity that I have come to find the greatest security. I have become convinced that the very contradictions in my life are in some ways signs of God's mercy to me. (Preface to *Poetry and the Christian*)

This liberation is the foundation of all the others. It liberates us *from* and *for*. It is the ultimate agreement to participate in *all* of life, to participate in the only world there is. From that vulnerable position, life itself will always be a good teacher. True participation in paradox liberates us *from* our own control towers and *for* the compelling and overarching vision of the Reign of God — where there are no liberals or conservatives. Here, the paradoxes — life and death, success and failure, loyalty to what is and risk for what needs to be — do not fight with one another, but lie in an endless embrace. We must penetrate behind them both — into the mystery that bears them both. Such activism is indestructible.

3

Tell Somebody

ESTHER ARMSTRONG

And Jesus said, "Woe to the world because of the things that cause people to sin! Such things must come, but woe to the one through whom they come!" (Matt. 18:7)

 "He was a real son of a bitch," spewed the shrill voice on the phone. A voice which continued to discharge venom, a voice I did not recognize until these harsh words were spoken: "We should have castrated the bastard while we had the chance."

I knew with this line that the voice had to be that of one more cousin saying those painful words, "Grandpa molested me when I was but a little girl." It was a line I have heard several times now, since the women of my generation began having cousins reunions a few years back.

And "son of a bitch" he was, that grandfather of mine. I have great compassion for this woman in her early sixties who was speaking for the very first time what I knew all too well to be one of the greatest tragedies in the lives of millions of young boys and girls. I knew the pain of getting in touch with a secret, long buried.

31

It was at the very first cousins gathering that I, waiting until most of the women had tipped a few too many, divulged that it was not Grandpa but the man we all called "uncle" who sexually molested me. My words that day hung like dew in the night air sobering up the most intoxicated among us. It seemed like forever before someone dared to respond.

"That was a long time ago! Can't you just move on with your life?" I might have wondered if the woman was speaking wisdom had it not been that her words were breaking through a stream of tears, and had it not been for the pounding of my own heart telling me that she too knew the meaning of victim.

The room that just a few minutes ago was overflowing with sick jokes and belly laughter now felt stuffed with dry, chalk-like air, air that even the bravest among us could not easily disturb.

"I think we should talk about it," whispered a soft voice from the corner. "I think we should talk about all the goddamn bastards who have raped and molested young victims."

I knew we wouldn't talk about such bastards on that day. I knew that time was needed between owning that such a horrid, life-altering experience had happened and bringing those dark memories to voice.

I also knew, from the stark silence in the room, from the tears that were being stifled, from the strangulating phlegm in some throats, that there were several present that day who would in their own time be courageous enough to say, "It also happened to me."

I wondered if the reason I had chosen to not attend this particular reunion from which the cousin was calling was because I was needed to listen to her from a distance. I know that sometimes words such as "real son of a bitch" need to be spoken into the air before they can be shared in an intimate circle. I knew all of this because it was this way for me and for the many who have bravely told me their stories.

I kept my secret for forty years. I kept it buried so deep that I did not, in fact, consciously remember it was even a part of my story.

Buried until that day when I literally vomited up the dark bile lying in my body for all those years.

I helped develop a program that would be taken to every third-grade classroom in a tri-county radius. It was a program that eventually went statewide. We called it "Tell Somebody." I was, on that dark day when the first ray of healing light appeared, training the volunteers who would take the program to the target audience.

I was about thirty minutes into the training when I said, "Let us always remember why we are doing this. We are seeking to teach young boys and girls the difference between good touch and bad touch, and when bad touch has happened, or they feel it is about to happen, that they should run and tell somebody. And if that first adult somebody doesn't believe them, they should tell another and another, until someone really hears and lets them know it was not their fault. We are doing this because we know that telling our stories is the first step toward healing. We must . . ."

I could not finish the sentence. My words were stuck in my vocal cords. I wrote a note on a piece of paper and handed it to my assistant suggesting we take a fifteen-minute break. I don't remember how I managed to get myself to the teachers' restroom, but I do remember lying in the fetal position around a toilet bowl. It was there that the secret I had buried all those years came whirling through my mind with such vivid force I felt as if what had happened those many years ago was happening all over again. I could hardly breathe. My body felt limp. My soul felt like it was being carried away, hovering somewhere over me, and I could not bring it back into my body. Everything felt surreal as the detailed images of that day I was molested rose up from a place very deep within. My head found its way to the toilet bowl, and for what seemed like forever I heaved those wretched memories out of my body and into the toilet.

My assistant finished the training, and I dragged my body out to the car knowing my own words, "you must tell somebody," were words of truth.

I knew this was also true for the cousin who was on the phone spewing forth, "He was a real son of a bitch." So I listened as prayerfully as possible, knowing her work had just begun.

4

Some

DANIEL BERRIGAN

Some stood up once   and sat down.
Some walked a mile   and walked away.
Some stood up twice   then sat down.
            I've had it, they said.
Some walked two miles   then walked away.
            It's too much, they cried.

Some stood and stood and stood.
They were taken for fools.
They were taken for being taken in.

Some walked and walked and walked.
They walked the earth.
They walked the waters.
They walked the air.

Why do you stand   they were asked, and
Why do you walk?

Because of the children, they said,
and Because of the heart, and
Because of the bread.
Because

The cause
Is the heart's beat
And the children born
And the risen bread.

5

Who, Me Tired?

CHRISTINE SCHENK

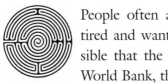 People often ask me, "Don't you ever get tired and want to give up? It seems impossible that the church (the government, the World Bank, the school board — insert selection of your choice) will ever change, and isn't the deck already stacked against you? Change happens so slowly, why bother?" When I hear this question, it reminds me of a quote by A. D. T. Whitney that has stayed with me since I first heard it as a young nun: "It is almost always when things are all blocked up and impossible that a happening comes. If you are sure you are looking and ready, that is all you need. God is turning the world around all the time."

It's not that I don't get tired of my work at Future-Church. I do. And I get discouraged too. But after ten years of education and advocacy in behalf of a more inclusive priesthood so that the Eucharist (in all its fullness of meaning) remains at the heart of our Catholic tradition, I can honestly say that the mission energizes me more than ever. In fact, the last ten years have provided the best schooling in faith that I have ever received.

You see, each time my fatigue and my discouragement threaten to overwhelm, a happening comes. Once when our computer was stolen shortly after the pope announced it was definitive all-time teaching forever that women could never be priests, I really thought I would lose it. To top it off, there was a raging snowstorm in Cleveland, and when I left the office at 9:00 p.m. my car battery had died. As I tromped through the snow to the nearby Catholic Worker house for help, I didn't disguise my sour, bitterly complaining mood: "Just what do you think you are doing anyhow, God," I asked angrily inside. At the Catholic Worker house, a young woman responded to my knock. She quickly got her car keys and proceeded to help me jump-start my car. When the engine was humming nicely, I thanked her and asked her name before she left. "Grace," she said simply. "My name is Grace."

A coincidence? Yes. But also "a happening," or, as Carl Jung would call it, a "synchronicity." (A "synchronicity" is a highfalutin word for grace manifested in the material plane right at the moment you need it most). Whatever you call it, it was what I needed that night to know that our mission at FutureChurch was part of the work of God's Spirit. I was not to give up because "Grace" would always be there to help me, and indeed grace has always been there. There are many other stories I could tell. Someday I would like to write them down in a book of "learnings" received in the Spirit's school of faith.

All of my stories have a similar theme. If our calling or mission really is from God, then God knows what to do to protect and nurture it. In the end the energy for doing good is God's own, not only or solely ours. We do good, because we must, because it is what gives us joy, because it gives joy to the God we love. We do not tire of doing good, because doing good is actually a positive addiction. It is participation in the goodness of God and is its own reward. When we tire, we return to the God place within to reconnect with the Spirit energy which leads and guides. A song based on Isaiah 40:28–31 says it well: "Trust in the Lord; you shall not tire. Serve you the Lord; you shall not weaken. For the Lord's own strength will uphold you. You shall renew your life and live." Let's hear it for God's own strength. Without it life is very boring. With it, who knows what can happen? "God is turning the world around all the time."

If tired, the wrong mission? Do with my passion

6

The Christian Call to Restorative Justice

A. COMPANION

 "Whoever did this will be brought to justice!" Hardly a day goes by that we don't see that angry promise in the newspaper or hear it on the evening news — whether it is voiced by the president in response to a terrorist act, the local sheriff at the scene of a crime, or a distraught victim or family member. Before you read any further, pause a moment and ask yourself what it means to be brought to justice. When you hear the demand for justice, what images come to your mind?

If your first responses include images of police, jail, and courtrooms, and your concepts primarily have to do with punishment, you are among the vast majority of Americans. Crime and punishment seem to go together like horse and buggy. For most of us, justice means going through the legal processes of accusation, arrest, establishing guilt, and imposing punishment, most often in the form of imprisonment, even execution.

If, however, your responses to the meaning of justice have to do with accepting responsibility, repenting, making restitution, and reestablishing well-being, you are on the path of restorative justice—the path that began when God banished Adam and Eve from the Garden, although Christians believe their estrangement was temporary and they would ultimately be brought back into God's healing embrace. This was brought about by the life, death, and resurrection of Jesus Christ—healing and restoration through God's radical and amazing grace.

The justice of God, upon which Christian faith and hope are dependent, is restorative justice. None of us has ever prayed, "Lord, give me what I deserve for my sins! Punish me to the full extent of the law!" But, when it comes to how we think about and do justice in regards to others, many of us who call upon God for mercy and compassion for ourselves experience no qualms at demanding "an eye for any eye" for "those who trespass against us." "Love one another *as* I have loved you," is the directive of the one who redeemed us from our sins—not because of our merit but because the justice of the cross is restorative.

◆ ◆ ◆

Restorative justice flows naturally from fundamental Christian principles and values: repentance, forgiveness, restitution, and rehabilitation. It is also the dynamic that animates Native American systems of justice, as well as those of other indigenous peoples. It has become the norm for the juvenile justice system in New Zealand, and, in the United States, Minnesota is a leader in integrating restorative justice approaches into its justice systems. For the most part, though, both the American justice systems and the American mind-set are based upon systems of justice that are retributive and punitive.

The faint voices of the restorers and healers around the world are drowned out by the cries for justice, revenge, and retaliation. This is true not only in the obvious places such as Israel, Palestine, and Northern Ireland, but also in U.S. national policies toward the "axis of evil," and even in our individual hearts as we wrestle with the hurts experienced every day within our families and friendships. So let us look more closely at what is meant by "retributive justice" and "restorative justice," how each works in practice, and how we can promote restorative justice in our hearts, homes, and homeland. The path from Eden to restorative justice is both a human challenge and a personal spiritual quest.

Retributive justice is premised upon returning hurt for hurt. Retributive systems of justice equate the crime committed to a violation of law and an offense against the state. The legal processes of retributive justice create an "us" versus "them" contest in which "the people" (represented by police, prosecutors, and judges) seek to prove guilt, then to punish it. For the most part, victims and offenders become observers as lawyers manipulate the truth and consequences as part of an elaborate game. At the end, justice is declared done if the procedural rules have been followed, guilt has been assigned, and punishment meted out. Most often, victims go home unhealed. Offenders are warehoused for a term of years, most often returning to society more dysfunctional than when they entered prison.

Restorative justice focuses upon healing hurts and restoring peace in hearts and communities. It starts with the presumption that victims and offenders are part of one family from which no one can be permanently excluded, and that what we do, good or evil, affects us all. Restorative systems approach crime as a violation of persons by persons. The legal processes of restorative models actively involve victims, offenders, their families and friends (and, perhaps, pastors, employers, or other community members) in the goal of healing the injuries and restoring well-being for all involved. In restorative justice, police, lawyers, judges, and others work with the victims and offenders toward a resolution that all accept as just. Restorative justice requires the offender to accept responsibility for the harm done and to make restitution. Besides healing and restitution for the victims, the conclusion may also mandate what the offender needs in order to heal and become rehabilitated, such as drug treatment counseling or vocational training. Punishment, when it is part of the sentence, is not punitive but purposeful toward the ultimate restoration of the offender.

Not every victim nor every offender is capable of pursuing restorative justice. For those who are, however, doing so provides the best potential for a win-win-win result, in which victim, offender, and the community find healing of the past and restored hope for the future. Hurts keep hurting — whether they are the victim's, the offender's, or the community's — until they are made redemptive: exchanged for healing and, if possible, reconciliation.

Retributive justice stays focused on what happened in the past. What good might be possible in the future is irrelevant. The restorative way begins with the harm done in the past, but measures justice done by the good that results in the future.

"I don't want your brother to die and I will do everything in my power to prevent it" were the compassionate words Bud Welch offered Timothy McVeigh's sister, Jennifer, while they cried together and he held her face in his hands. Welch's daughter, Julie, was killed in the Oklahoma City bombing. He went through a long period of rage, craving revenge, before he allowed himself to feel the healing of forgiveness and was able to reach out "as family" to Jennifer, as innocent as Julie and injured to her depths, too. Even now, Bud Welch tours the country speaking against the death penalty.

International attention focused on Laramie, Wyoming, in 1998, after Aaron J. McKinney and an accomplice lured Matthew Shepard from a bar, drove out of town, tied him to a fence, savagely beat him, and left him to die because he was a homosexual. In the courtroom, as the jury was preparing to decide whether to impose the death penalty, many wept as Matthew's father, Dennis, spoke lovingly of his son as a person who could only see the good in others and who had been "my hero, now gone forever." Then, turning to Matthew's killer, he stunned the courtroom with: "Mr. McKinney, I give you life in memory of the one who no longer lives." The Shepards had requested the prosecutor not to seek the death penalty, and life in prison without possibility of parole was imposed instead.

Freeing ourselves from locked-in mind-sets is not easy. Changing the ways we see, think, and do things takes time. But the awe-inspiring witness of Bud Welch and Dennis and Judy Shepard prove that it is possible. There are not only spiritual and humane considerations, but also many practical, fiscal, and political reasons to pursue restorative approaches to justice. With 2 million Americans incarcerated or on parole or probation, and with a 67 percent recidivism rate after incarceration, even those who run the misnamed "corrections" systems acknowledge building more prisons is not the answer. "An eye for an eye, a tooth for a tooth" demeans victim, offender, and society, and perpetuates the cycle of violence and harm it fruitlessly seeks to eradicate.

Japan utilizes parallel restorative and retributive systems. Depending upon the nature of the crime, the offender's willingness to acknowledge guilt, express remorse, and make compensation, and the victim's willingness to receive compensation and to pardon, the determination is made whether to pursue a restorative or retributive process. When the victim and offender can agree to a just resolution, punishment is usually lenient. Incarceration is the exception, rather than the norm, and long-term imprisonment is used only for the most unusual cases. Japan has a very low crime rate.

Since 1989, New Zealand's juvenile justice system has totally built upon the restorative principles followed by the native Maoris. All juvenile facilities have been closed, except a few for youth who commit horrendous crimes, but even in them, the emphasis is on education, therapy, and skill development. For those who do not accept responsibility for their crimes, a parallel traditional system is in place.

Minnesota's Carver County Sheriff's Department and Woodbury City Police Department set up family group conferencing before or after sentencing in juvenile court (or as an alternative to it). The process brings together victims, offenders, the families of both, and other community resource persons to talk about how the crime has affected their lives and to decide how the harm done might be repaired.

New York, Arizona, Missouri, and California are among the states moving from incarceration for minor first- and second-offense drug crimes to treatment of the addiction that leads to robbery and theft. The goal is to rehabilitate and restore addicts, not to punish addiction.

In California, "Volunteers in Parole" matches attorneys and judges as mentors for parolees who have been discerned as most determined to change their lives. The program is cosponsored by the state bar of California, county bar associations, and the state department of corrections. Its goal is to break the cycle of recidivism and to restore parolees as contributing members of society.

◆ ◆ ◆

The path and promise that began in the Garden, the story of God's relationship with humanity, is rightly called "salvation history." In the biblical stories of wandering and restoration, punishment for sin has as its purpose not revenge, but redemption. Restoration is the goal. And, when an individual or the nation repents and turns again to God, it is the father of the prodigal son who races out to embrace and heal. These stories are not just those of our faith ancestors, but they are yours and mine, as well. They are not stories of abandonment but stories of hope. To do restorative justice does not mean that those who break the law and harm the peace of the community should not be held accountable, nor does it mean there should not be punishment, including prison for the small numbers who truly threaten the safety of the community. It does mean, however, that we refuse to equate punishment with justice, and justice with prison.

Precisely because we are Christians who have been redeemed by the restorative justice of God in spite of our many sins and failings, we are obligated to practice restorative justice in our homes and personal relationships and to speak the truth to legislators and neighbors that even one who harms us remains one of us. The redemptive journey that began at the closed gates of Eden does not end for any of us until the gates of the kingdom — opened wide by radical and amazing grace.

7

Eyes That See

AARON FROEHLICH

Aaron spent April 15–30, 2002, in Israel and the West Bank as a participant on an emergency delegation with Christian Peacemaker Teams (CPT, www.cpt.org/). He was one of fourteen participants who traveled to various areas of the West Bank, including Nablus, Hebron, Bethlehem, and Ramallah, engaging in nonviolent actions, listening to stories, and ministering through presence.

 Contemplating death at thirty-six thousand feet as you prepare to descend into a war zone has a way of bringing perspective to your life. Over and over, I turned round my reasoning for making a journey to Israel and the West Bank. What if I don't make it home? How much do I believe in nonviolence? What sacrifices am I willing to make for a better world for my son? There was a young Israeli boy, days older than my son, David, sleeping peacefully on his father's chest. As I looked at him, I marveled at how much he reminded me of David. My joy turned to sorrow as I imagined how different their lives would be.

Days before, my wife, Celeste, received an e-mail calling for a stronger international presence in the West Bank. "Would we be crazy to look into it?" she asked. Our hearts were breaking each morning as we read about the suffering in the land that we had grown to love so deeply while living there in 1997–98. It was paralyzing to be sitting thousands of miles away, with only the Internet to help us sift through the misinformation in the American media.

In the words of CPT, "until people committed to nonviolence are willing to take the same risks for peace that soldiers are willing to take for war, people will always choose violence as the most viable solution to their problems." CPT is a Mennonite-, Quaker-, and Brethren-sponsored organization committed to nonviolent intervention in situations of violent conflict. Their experience has demonstrated that teams of four to six people trained in the skills of documentation, observation, nonviolent intervention, and various ministries of presence — including patience — can make a striking difference in explosive situations. In a moment of clarity that I would question many times in the following weeks, Celeste and I decided that God was calling our family to take a risk for nonviolence.

On Holy Ground

"Why are you coming to Israel? Don't you know there is a war here?" My answer was ready after being asked these same questions at least ten times by six different airport security personnel who had interrogated me. "Listen, I'm just here on vacation. I'm going to stay as far away from the West Bank as possible," came my carefully rehearsed reply.

Would they believe me, or would I be turned away on the next plane like the group of European doctors had been the day before? The deeper questions had already been asked, though not answered. Will I ever sing "Rise and Shine" again to David's early morning giggles? Am I really ready to give my life for nonviolence?

If the prospect of death has a way of making life particularly relevant, perhaps the inverse is true as well: when life begins to feel irrelevant, death seems to carry little meaning. This point was hammered home as I sat on a couch next to a forty-five-year-old man in Nablus. Five other CPT emergency delegates and I had just made the arduous journey from Jerusalem to Nablus, a mere forty miles that took us eight hours. Our circuitous path had taken three taxis and a long hike through the rolling Samarian hillsides, where we had successfully avoided the Israeli tanks still roaming the streets and hilltops. The residents of Nablus had been confined to their homes for almost three weeks when we arrived.

The man sitting next to me spoke fluent English and began telling us about his work as a translator for the U.S. Army in Saudi Arabia. After fifteen years of successful work, he returned to Palestine with his wife and four children because he believed in the peace process. He thought it would bring the Palestinians a state. "I can't even look into my children's eyes right now," he shared. "They don't blame me, but I can't help but blame myself."

The man's niece was one of the recent suicide bombers. She was young, bright, and about to graduate from university. The moment that put her over the edge was when a young family in labor was stopped at a checkpoint. As often happens in the West Bank, the couple was refused passage under the pretense of road closures. What made this situation "newsworthy," however, was that the husband and brother were shot and killed in front of the laboring woman. "What makes a suicide bomber?" her uncle asked me. "There is no difference between life and death here."

Over the two-week period we spent in the West Bank, the overused word "terror" began to take on a new meaning for me. Palestinians generally detest the word as they hear the Israeli army use phrases like "rooting out the terrorist infrastructure" to justify their state-sponsored violence — violence which often targets Palestinian civilians in order to achieve Israeli aims. Witnessing the monumental destruction typified by Nablus and Jenin, I can't help but agree. The grossly misleading thing about the use of the word "terror" by the Israelis and the international media is that it ignores, perhaps even covers up, the very clear and consistent targeting of civilian and municipal infrastructure by the Israeli army, such as the Palestinian Authority Ministry of Health and Ministry of Education. In my opinion, this is not only malicious, but also a form of terror. Certainly, one would be hard-pressed to argue that the destruction of water lines, computers, children's art centers, and municipal buildings has made the Israelis any more "secure." In fact, the real Israeli objective of the recent reinvasions seems to have been to destroy the infrastructure for a viable Palestinian state.

Perhaps even more tragic than the destruction of buildings, however, is the destruction of Palestinian hope. Weeks of endless curfew have left the people traumatized all over again. During the first three weeks of nearly continuous curfew, people could hardly sleep at night as the tanks roamed the streets, firing at will. Many families would take turns staying up to warn the others if the soldiers were coming. One young man we talked with had to dodge snipers in order to get food from the refrigerator on his own porch.

In Ramallah, we met with Diana, principal of the Quaker elementary school, who helped us understand the impact of the reinvasion. On their first day back to school, Diana was saddened but not surprised to see that the children were all playing "tanks" in the schoolyard. She decided to gather everyone together to talk about their experiences and to let the kids know that it is okay to be afraid. Some children told their stories in the microphone. Then they spent their class time talking in small groups about what had happened to them. Some of these elementary school children are now wetting their pants on a regular basis. Most are afraid to sleep alone. "My daughter is fifteen, and she is now sleeping next to me," mourned Diana. "I ask myself, what have I been doing for twenty-five years, teaching the kids about nonviolence? How can they understand something like this?"

Diana then told us a story. During the Gulf War, an Israeli tank passed by their house, and Diana's five-year-old daughter asked, "Mommy, what is this soldier doing? Do they drink? Do soldiers eat?" Diana realized that her daughter, whose name means "hope" in Arabic, didn't understand that soldiers were human beings.

Days later, the soldiers came to her house to search it. Brazenly, Diana asked one of them, "Will you sit down and talk to my daughter?" He looked at her with surprise and annoyance. "No, I'm serious. You see, my daughter thinks you are not a real human being. I want you to sit down and let her touch your hand — let her feel your hand. I want her to know that you are a person just like her." The soldier sat down and said slowly, "I am a doctor." He then proceeded to tell them about his life — his family, his children, his call back to duty as a reservist. "For that time, we were just human beings, sitting together talking to one another," said Diana.

As she spoke, Diana's courage and wisdom amazed me. Yet the passing years have been hard on her. Diana now fears for her life, because she was interviewed on Arabic television saying, "They are brutal," about the soldiers who tore apart her house while she was away taking care of her mother. In expectation of the search, Diana left her keys with the neighbor. When the soldiers arrived, they told the neighbors, "We don't need keys" as they shot through the door. Now Diana questions the very meaning of her life's work for nonviolent education. "I keep asking myself, 'Why? Why?' They could have avoided this! I'm not mad at the Israelis as much as I am mad at human beings. Why do we do this?"

In an affirmation to herself as well as to us, Diana said, "We have to hold on to hope." Her sincerity pierced my heart. "We must find that small space for hope in our hearts and protect it." She ended by talking about the hope that she is holding on to. Sadly, it's not for herself. "I don't want this life, this terror, anymore. I remember, as a young child, school being closed because of the demonstrations and rock throwing. Today, little has changed. I don't want this for my children. I hope for a better world, a different world. If not for us, at least for our children."

Black and White?

A day after walking through the torn streets of Ramallah and meeting Diana, my worldview was stretched yet again as I talked with Daniel Rossing, a dear Jewish-Israeli friend and mentor. When I lived in Israel in the late 1990s, it was Daniel who had originally helped me see beyond the black/white, us/them perceptions of the Middle East. Daniel, who worked in interreligious conflict resolution for many years, passionately experiences the world through infinite shades of gray.

Moments after we saw each other again for the first time in years, Daniel's tone turned from joyful to serious. "I have to warn you," he said as we rode together away from Jerusalem in his car, "last month a neighbor was shot at as he drove home. He wasn't hurt, but there were more than twenty bullet holes in his car." Daniel lives in a small Israeli neighborhood in the Judean hills.

"My daughters refuse to come this summer," he shared as we drove together in the dark. Knowing how deeply he cares for his young teenage daughters, who live in Amsterdam, I felt the sadness of his statement sink in. "They don't even know about the attack on my neighbor, but their school has been receiving threats, and they are terrified. You can't imagine what it is like to wake up every night with nightmares about the death of my children."

"You wouldn't believe how scared everyone is," sighed Daniel, as we sat in a long line of cars waiting to park at the grocery store. Each car had to be searched for bombs before entering the parking garage. "Our country is so deeply traumatized, and now there's all this anti-Semitism in Europe. . . ."

During the twenty-four hours I spent with Daniel, my mind was stretched time and again. We laughed, we argued, we cried — we tried to listen to a narrative larger than our own. "Everyone wants to be right," remarked Daniel, "but you know, there is a difference between being right and being wise." His statement struck me to the core. I thought back to the action our group did in Bethlehem. About thirty-five of us marched together through the silent streets toward the Church of the Nativity. Because we were "internationals," the curfew did not directly apply to us. About a hundred meters from Nativity Square, we were stopped by soldiers in the narrow streets and refused passage. After more than an hour of unsuccessful negotiating and pleading, we discovered that our presence might be keeping some of the Palestinians living around us from taking advantage of the short lift in curfew. Immediately, we decided to end our protest and walk away from the church. Under international law and the Geneva Conventions, we had a "right" to care for the sick and wounded. But we chose to do what was wise, given that this was the first lift in curfew in more than three weeks for some of the families around the church.

"What are you doing here, Aaron?" asked Daniel, cutting to the chase. "How many people has your country killed in Afghanistan? What are you doing about that? Don't you realize how hypocritical you seem?" I wanted to lash out at Daniel: to tell him about how angry I have felt about the U.S. attack on Afghanistan, to tell him about all the terrible things that I had witnessed over my two weeks in the West Bank, to remind him that two wrongs do not make a right. But that was precisely his point — that there is a difference between what is right and what is wise. "When you have a protest in Washington, D.C., and some are carrying Israeli flags with swastikas on them, don't you realize that you are making my struggle for peace here more difficult? Is that an intelligent way to bring about peace in the Middle East?"

Daniel's words, like Diana's and those of the man in Nablus, have remained with me since returning from my journey. The three of them call me daily to a deeper integrity and accountability. They remind me to constantly question what I believe is true, because so often my small mind wants to cling to simple answers and avoid ambiguity.

An Invitation to Living Water

The road from Nablus to the Balata refugee camp takes you past the biblical site of Jacob's well. As we walked past this site one day, a member of the group reminded us that this was also where Jesus asked the Samaritan woman for water at the well (John 4:7–42). "Everyone who drinks of this water will be thirsty again, but those who drink of the water that I will give them will never be thirsty." Ironically, just meters past this holy site live thousands of refugees, many of whom are struggling without food and water following the heavy shelling of their camp.

The Gospel story continues with the Samaritan woman returning to the city to tell people that she has met the Messiah, "for he has told me everything I have ever done." Her "living water" came in a surprising form: seeing everything she had ever done — seeing through her own personal narrative of lies. Looking back over my life, I realize the great challenge it has been to see "everything I have ever done."

In today's world, Jesus' message of "seeing" is as needed as ever. "Forgive them, Abba, for they know not what they do," said Jesus. This was not an idle statement, but one made at the point of deepest agony and suffering. Perhaps Jesus' greatest accomplishment was inviting people to see the world with new eyes — eyes that are unable to gloss over the oppression that we cause and the mistakes that we make, eyes that see oppression but refuse to hate the oppressor.

The media thrives on black and white, terrorism versus democracy, good versus evil stories. The real "terror" of the twenty-first century is not suicide bombs or chemical warfare, but that self-righteous, well-meaning people on all sides continue to perpetrate "sacred violence" in God's name rather than drink from the living water that sees truth and refuses blame. We so easily forget that the United States, our beloved protagonist of freedom and democracy, continues to fund and support oppressive regimes worldwide. We fail to see that our own hands are still stained with the blood of the Native Americans. How do we respond to Sharon's statement to Powell last year: "We learn a lot from you Americans; this is how you moved West"? Most of us simply look for the "truth" that supports our own vision of goodness, ignoring that we have little moral ground to stand on as our stones are raised high, ready to be thrown at the problem.

How do we not avert our eyes, but really see the impact of U.S. policy in the Middle East and elsewhere? Can we bear to struggle with the questions such seeing raises? What does it mean to pay taxes in a country where a third of our foreign aid goes to Israel to fund the perpetuation of a brutal thirty-five-year occupation — not to mention funding our own questionable war on terrorism? Can we see how the relationships of communities in our own streets reverberate in the world? Can we seek to be a healing presence as we listen to the deep fear and anger growing both for Jewish Americans and Arab Americans? What does it mean to see the relationship between the gas we pump and the blood spilled in the Middle East? In my daily life, do I really strive to help others to see these questions as well?

Holding on to Hope

The hugs and smiles I received from Celeste and David as I returned to the Albuquerque airport were the best of my life. Yet what felt like the end to my journey was really just the beginning. Since then, my struggle to understand and communicate my experience has continued. For me, it will probably never be easy, because I believe in Daniel's call to be wise more than right. I want my life, and death, to have meaning. And most of all, I want to hold on to hope — believing that my small efforts can make a difference in our world. It's not my place to search for the "solution," or to lead anyone else there either; my call is to be faithful to God's ongoing incarnation in my life, and to walk forward with a growing commitment to see with new eyes and live with greater integrity.

8

I Am the Way, the Truth, and the Life

EDWINA GATELY

I used to think that following Jesus was all rather noble and exciting and that if one really got on with it and flung oneself into the arena of Justice and Mission, one might well emerge shrouded in light and ecstasy. As a young woman, I'd read hundreds of stories about saints and martyrs who followed the Way, the Truth, and the Life and, in spite of the myriad struggles en route, still emerged looking seraphic and blissful in the religious art that portrayed them for all generations to come. Alas, such comforting notions began to fade rapidly as I plodded further and further in pursuit of the Way, the Truth, and the Life.

My first major foray along the path led me to Uganda, East Africa, as a zealous and faith-filled lay missionary intent on sharing my faith and gifts with the poor folks I was to find there. The God I took with me was the white, male, Catholic (and British) God whom I knew, without a doubt, was (like my church) the One and Only True One.

It was quite a shock to discover that God had got to Africa before me! As time passed, I began to perceive God in the eyes of the people whom I had gone to save. I saw God's grace reflected in their hospitality and openness to me — a foreign white woman who couldn't even speak their language! I discovered in Africa that God was big — brown and white, male and female. God was in the generosity of the people who shared the little they had with me; God was in the banana plantations and in the throbbing of the drums echoing across the awesome savanna. God, I came to realize, would not, could not, fit into the rather nice solid box I had put God into.

Following Jesus along the bumpy way into a cross-cultural experience quickly dispelled my presumptuous notions about who God was and what God looked like. I was left with a big empty space: exposed to a different culture and a different way of being church (much noisier, disorganized, and distinctly more cheerful than church at home — nobody batted an eyelid at the hens wandering across the sanctuary, or even the occasional goat). I came to understand that God was stretching my hitherto limited notion of church and truth. The people in Africa whom I had gone to help became my teachers, and their lesson for me was that I was, and would always be, en route along the Way in search of Truth and Life.

Years later (still plodding along with a little bit of light and a little bit of salt and a little bit of yeast) I found myself sitting in an old trailer in the woods responding to a rather ridiculous but very certain call to do nothing but listen. This experience was distinctly countercultural in a society where productivity and results are priorities and expectations for all able-bodied folks. Sitting in a silent and eremitical environment waiting to be visited by the Word of God was actually rather tedious — not at all the inspiring and grace-filled experience I had fondly hoped for. The Way, the Truth, and the Life was proving, it seemed to me, positively elusive and uninspiring. Nevertheless, I waited and waited and waited. I knew I was supposed to be there doing nothing. It was all rather dark and bleak for a lot of the time and I often felt guilty because I was not doing anything at all to save the world or build the realm of God. But I still stayed there — expectant, like a woman hoping to give birth.

It was not until the ninth month that I began to become conscious of a call. It was a call that seemed to surface from a deep, silent part of me. Years later I reflected on how I could never have heard God's whisper had I not first been faithful to the silence and the waiting. Life, it occurred to me, emerged from darkness and stillness. This then was indeed an essential experience of following the Way and the Truth. The call itself was certainly not one I would have heard amid the normal noise and activity of day-to-day life. It was the call to urban ministry, which led me to the streets of Chicago, where I was to encounter women involved in a lifestyle of prostitution, drug addicts, and people who were homeless.

Perhaps it was quite understandable that they welcomed me with an invitation to "F— off." Once again I was having problems with the Way, the Truth, and the Life. . . . I was, after all, only *on* the streets because I had listened and followed! But clearly I was not welcome! It was in fact months before I began to experience a vague kind of acceptance from the people I believed I was sent to love and serve.

They eventually got used to me hanging around — loitering as they did, down the alleys and side streets. They began to ask me for small favors — "Watch out for the cops. . . ." "Got a cigarette?" Then, little by little, they began to share bits of their life stories with me — all broken and violent and painful. Almost all of them had been victims of some form of childhood violence. I felt blessed by their sharing and their trust. The initial silence, darkness, and waiting began to bear fruit in a ministry of hospitality, healing, and outreach. I experienced God's grace flowing on the streets of Chicago, and I was deeply grateful for the privilege of being received into the lives of the brokenhearted.

Since then I have been a witness to many resurrections. Through coming to know and love so many broken people on the Way, I have also come to be part of their hopes and dreams for new Life. It seems to me that God seduces us to risky places in order to experience miracles we would not otherwise see. I have seen women whose lives were an endless catalogue of abuse and violence begin to believe that maybe they could be healed, maybe they could live again, maybe there was hope for them. I have walked with them on their so difficult journeys from hell to new life, and I am left amazed and awed at their courage and spirit. The words from scripture "For s/he was dead and has come to life, was lost and is found" have for me taken on a profound and living significance.

Perhaps the words of one woman who struggled to leave behind twenty years of prostitution and drug addiction best illustrate the miracles we are invited to behold as we follow the Way, the Truth, and the Life: "Today I am no longer homeless. I no longer dress, act, or behave like a prostitute. Today I am a proud parent. Today I am registered in college to prepare for a career in addictions counseling. Today I am employed at a center serving the homeless. Most of all, I love myself. I no longer hide behind a street name. Today my life is a gift from a Power greater than myself." That Power is, indeed, the Way, the Truth, and the Life.

9

Edifying Tales of Nonviolence

WALTER WINK

Stories of nonviolence are instructive. Millions of years of violence have ill prepared us for nonviolent reactions. We need such stories to stretch our imaginations. We need to rehearse situations that might arise so as to avoid being caught unprepared. When we see how other people were able to rise to the challenge of nonviolent reactions, we are enabled to act creatively as well, but there is another reason to tell these stories. They are, with few exceptions, surprising, interesting, even amazing in their sheer originality. Here are a few of my favorites. Enjoy.

♦ ♦ ♦

South African archbishop Desmond Tutu walked by a construction site on a temporary sidewalk the width of one person. A white man appeared at the other end, recognized Tutu, and said, "I don't make way for gorillas." At which Tutu stepped aside, made a deep sweeping gesture, and said, "Ah, yes, but I do."

◆ ◆ ◆

During the struggle of Solidarity in Poland, one group dressed in Santa Claus outfits and distributed scarce sanitary napkins to women as a way of dramatizing the difficulty of obtaining essentials. When these Santas were arrested, other Santas showed up at jail insisting that the others were frauds, that they were the real Santas.

◆ ◆ ◆

Chinese students, forbidden to demonstrate against government policy, donned masks of the Communist leadership and carried signs reading: "Support Martial Law," "Support Dictatorship," "Support Inflation." (I especially like this one. It has such suggestive possibilities. How about, for example, "Give tax breaks to the rich." Or, "Collateral damage ain't nothin'.")

◆ ◆ ◆

A squatter community in South Africa found its shelter infested with lice. When the authorities refused to fumigate it, the leadership committee took bags of lice-infested blankets to the administrator's office and dumped them on his floor. They got immediate action.

◆ ◆ ◆

Montana, long known as "Big Sky" territory, is vast and beautiful. One might assume there is room enough for everyone. Yet over the last decade the five-state area of Washington, Oregon, Wyoming, Idaho, and Montana has been designated a "white homeland" for the Aryan Nation. White supremacist groups have targeted nonwhites,

Jews, gays, and lesbians. In Billings, Montana, there were many hate crimes, including the desecration of a Jewish cemetery, threatening phone calls to Jewish citizens, and swastikas painted on the home of an interracial couple. But it was something else that activated the people of faith and good will throughout the entire community.

On December 2, 1993, a brick was thrown through five-year-old Isaac Schnitzer's bedroom window. The brick and shards of glass were strewn all over the child's bed. The reason? A menorah and other symbols of Jewish faith were stenciled on the glass as part of the family's Hanukkah celebrations. The account of the incident in the *Billings Gazette* the next day described Isaac's mother, Tammie Schnitzer, as being troubled by the advice she got from the investigating officer. He suggested she remove the symbols. How would she explain this to her son? Another mother in Billings was deeply touched by that question. She tried to imagine explaining to her children that they couldn't have a Christmas tree in the window, because it wasn't safe. She remembered what happened when Hitler ordered the king of Denmark to force all Danish Jews to wear Stars of David. The order was never carried out, because the king himself and many other Danes chose to wear the yellow stars. The Nazis lost the ability to find their "enemies."

There are several dozen Jewish families in Billings. This kind of tactic could effectively deter violence if enough people got involved. So Margaret McDonald phoned her pastor, Rev. Keith Torney at First Congregational United Church of Christ, and asked what he thought of having Sunday School children make paper cut-out menorahs for their own windows. The following week hundreds of menorahs appeared in the windows of Christian homes. When asked about the danger of this action, Police Chief Wayne Inman told callers, "There's greater risk in not doing it." By the end of the week at least six thousand homes (some accounts estimated up to ten thousand) were decorated with menorahs.

A sporting goods store got involved by displaying "Not in Our Town! No hate, No violence, Peace on Earth," on its large billboard. Someone shot at it. Townspeople organized a vigil outside the synagogue during Sabbath services. That same night bricks and bullets shattered windows at Central Catholic High School, where an electric marquee read "Happy Hanukkah to our Jewish friends." The cat of a family with a menorah was killed with an arrow. Six non-Jewish families had their car and house windows shattered. One car had a note that said "Jew lover."

Eventually these incidents waned, but people continued in their efforts to support one another against hate crimes. During the Passover holiday, 250 Christians joined their Jewish brothers and sisters in a traditional seder. New friendships formed, new traditions started, and greater mutual understanding and respect have been achieved. The next winter families all over Billings took out their menorahs to reaffirm their commitment to peace and religious tolerance.

◆ ◆ ◆

An elderly South African woman carries religious tracts written in the thirteen languages of South Africa and approaches people, asks what language they speak, and hands them one of her tracts. Invariably they are pleased that someone would have gone to the trouble to give out tracts in their own tongue. A problem arose at the office where she picks up her social security check. Robbers would simply wait around outside and seize the checks almost as the people emerged. She solved the problem by putting her check under her stack of tracts, walking straight up to the most threatening robbers, and asking, "What language do you speak?" Pleased, they take their tract and go away.

◆ ◆ ◆

One of my favorite stories was told to me by the mother of the protagonist. It seems that this kid's school bus was being terrorized by a big kid, and the driver did nothing about it. Our hero, it turns out, had chronic sinusitis, and his nose ran all the time. One day he had had enough. Standing up, he blew his right hand full of snot and approached the bully saying, "I want to shake the hand of a real bully." The bully, his eyes fixed on that hand, slowly backed up until he was at the back of the bus. That was the end of his career as a bully, because that nose was always at the ready.

◆ ◆ ◆

A Philadelphia woman was walking home after dark carrying two bags of groceries. She became aware that someone was coming up behind here. Just as the footsteps reached her, she spun around and shoved the bags into the young man's arms, saying, "Thank goodness you've come! I couldn't have carried these groceries any longer." The man carried her bags to her house, handed them back, and disappeared.

◆ ◆ ◆

The next two stories I heard from Arun Gandhi, the grandson of the architect of Indian independence. The great Gandhi was only thirteen when he was married. He had no idea how to go about being a husband, so he got some books from the library, all of which were by male chauvinists who said that he had to assert his authority over his wife. So that night he told his wife that she couldn't leave the house without his permission. She said nothing and went to bed. The next day she went about her daily tasks at the market, temple, and so forth. When he realized what she was doing, he confronted her. Without rancor, she quietly said, "I was raised to believe that we must obey our elders. Do you want me to tell your mother that I can't obey her any more?" That settled that. This would have been one of his first experiences of nonviolent direct action, in this case, used against him.

During one of the family's stays in South Africa, Arun drove his father (this would have been Gandhi's son) into Durban. Having been strictly charged to return by five o'clock, Arun drove the car to be repaired and then raced to the theater, which was showing a John Wayne double feature. He became so engrossed that he lost all track of time. The movie ended at 5:30. He rushed to the garage, got the car, and drove to pick up his father. His father, anxious that he hadn't returned on time, asked why he was so late. Arun replied that the car wasn't ready. But his father had already called the garage. "I am trying to understand what I did wrong as a parent that you would feel you had to lie to me. So I am going to walk the eighteen miles home while I try to figure out how I failed." So without even taking off his dress coat and tie, he started walking, suit, dress shoes, and all. As evening fell it became pitch dark. Arun crept along in the car behind his father. During that interminable drive, Arun decided he would never, ever, tell a lie again. The goal of Arun Gandhi's parents was not to punish, or to humiliate, or to break their children's spirits, but to transform them. To that end they would fast when their children did wrong. They would feed their children, but refuse to eat themselves, doing penance for their failure to raise their children right.

◆ ◆ ◆

A Native American grandfather was talking to his grandson about the tragedy on September 11. He said, "I feel as if I have two wolves fighting in my heart. One wolf is vengeful, angry, and violent. The other one is loving and compassionate." The grandon asked, "Which wolf will win the fight in your heart?" The grandfather answered, "The one I feed."

◆ ◆ ◆

Women and nonviolence have a long history together. Women carried out the first act of civil disobedience in recorded history, when two Hebrew midwives, Shiphrah and Puah, violated the Egyptian Pharaoh's command to kill all male Hebrew babies, thus preserving the life of the future liberator, Moses (Exod. 1–2). The Greek playwright Sophocles portrayed Antigone burying her brother in defiance of the king's command. Another Greek playwright,

Aristophanes, depicted women on both sides stopping a war by withholding sex from their husband-soldiers.

♦ ♦ ♦

Withholding sex has been used to great effect many times. At the beginning of the seventeenth century the women of the Iroquois Indian nation conducted the "first feminist rebellion in the U.S." Unless the men conceded to them the power to decide upon war and peace, there would be no more lovemaking and childbearing. Thus they successfully curbed their husbands' warfare. More recently, women in (then) Southern Rhodesia demanded that their husbands stop an outbreak of bombings and explosions or lose all marital rights.

♦ ♦ ♦

At other times, protest has moved out of the privacy of the bedroom and overflowed into the streets. Around 46 B.C.E. Herod, the governor of Galilee, murdered the insurrectionist Ezekias and many of his fellow conspirators without due process of law. In protest, "every day in the temple the mothers of the men who had been executed begged the king and the people to have Herod condemned" — a tactic employed in our time in Cuba under the dictator Batista, in Argentina by the "Mothers of the Plaza de Mayo," and in El Salvador and the Soviet Union.

♦ ♦ ♦

One of the earliest strikes was pioneered by women in 1818, when hospital laundresses in Valencia, Venezuela, struck to demand back pay. Women played critical roles in the Underground Railroad, helping slaves escape to freedom in the American North or Canada. Women were major figures in the nineteenth-century abolitionist movement, the temperance movement, and the anti-war movement. In 1871, women in Paris blocked cannons and stood between Prussian and Parisian troops. In 1878, Kusunose Kita in Shihoku, Japan, protested having to pay taxes while being denied the vote as a woman. Women in New Zealand achieved suffrage in 1893, and in Australia in 1902. After a seventy-five year struggle, women finally won the right to vote in the United States in 1920.

◆ ◆ ◆

In 1892, Ida B. Wells-Barnett led a mass boycott followed by a mass exodus from Memphis to northern cities to protest lynchings and discrimination against blacks. Whole congregations left — over two thousand people in two months. And in 1955, Rosa Parks triggered the civil rights movement in Montgomery, Alabama, when she refused to go to the back of the bus.

◆ ◆ ◆

Mairead Corrigan and Betty Williams received the Nobel Peace Prize for their efforts at nonviolent reconciliation in Northern Ireland. Another Nobel laureate, Aung San Suu Kyi, has continued to lead a democracy movement in Myanmar from captivity in her home (already, as of this writing, she has been under house arrest for a decade). And Nobel laureate Rigoberta Menchú risked her life day after day to liberate Guatemala from a repressive military government. Other women Nobel peace laureates include

Jane Addams, Baroness von Suttner, Alva Myrdal, Edith Greene Blach, and Jody Williams.

◆ ◆ ◆

In Peruvian barrios, where the homes are crowded tightly together and their walls provide little by way of privacy, the women have found a brilliant way to counter the age-long practice of male violence toward wives. When the beating starts, all the neighboring women begin beating on pots and pans, till the husband is shamed into stopping. And the threat of future bangings has a wonderfully restraining effect. In Africa, when a woman has been mistreated by her man, she goes to a women's club to which she belongs and tells the other women about it. The women go to the village square with their rhythm instruments. There, they play and sing the story of the cruelty. Before long, the whole village knows what the husband has done.

◆ ◆ ◆

Not long after Pontius Pilate was appointed procurator in Judea (26 C.E.), he introduced into Jerusalem by night "the busts of the emperor that were attached to the military standards," which Jews regarded as idols and thus a desecration of the holy city. Crowds of Jews rushed to Pilate's headquarters in Caesarea to implore him to remove the standards. When he refused, they fell prostrate on the ground and remained there for five days and nights. On the sixth day, Pilate summoned the multitude to the stadium on the pretext of giving them an answer. Instead, they found themselves surrounded by soldiers, three deep.

Pilate signaled to the soldiers to draw their swords. Thereupon the Jews, as by concerted action, flung themselves in a body on the ground, extended their necks, and exclaimed that they were ready to die rather than to transgress the law. Overcome with astonishment at such intense religious zeal, Pilate gave orders for the immediate removal of the standards from Jerusalem.

◆ ◆ ◆

Occasionally, holy stripping of the kind that Jesus describes (Matt. 5:40) is literally enacted. Shortly before the end of apartheid in South Africa, bulldozers and police arrived at a squatters' camp and announced to the few women there (the rest having gone to work) that they had five minutes to clear out their few belongings before the camp would be demolished. The black women, perhaps sensing the prudery of these largely rural Calvinist Afrikaners, stood in front of the bulldozers and stripped off all their clothing. The police turned and fled. To the best of my knowledge, they never came back.

◆ ◆ ◆

What makes the mugger, the bully, or the soldier so vulnerable is the element of surprise. They have a picture in their heads of what is about to happen. A violent or hostile response, or one of panic or helplessness, reinforces the assailant's expectations. When their potential victim fails to respond as expected, the aggressor is thrown off balance. Surprise tends to diffuse hostility, says Angie O'Gorman. When the victim focuses on what causes wonder, a desire to imitate tends to occur, a form of positive mimesis that creates in the assailant a strong new impulse incompatible with the violent tendency.

One night O'Gorman was awakened by an intruder in her room. "I asked him what time it was. He answered. That was a good sign. I commented that his watch and the clock on my night table had different times. His said 2:30, mine said 2:45. I had just set mine. I hoped that his watch wasn't broken. When had he last set it? He answered. I answered. The time seemed endless. When the atmosphere began to calm a little, I asked him how he had gotten into the house. He'd broken through the glass in the back door. I told him that presented me with a problem as I did not have the money to buy new glass. He talked about some financial difficulties of his own. He talked until we were no longer strangers and I felt it was safe to ask him to leave. He didn't want to; said he had no place to go. Knowing I did not have the physical power to force him out, I told him firmly but respectfully, as equal to equal, that I would give him a clean set of sheets, but he would have to make his own bed downstairs. He went downstairs and I sat up in bed, wide awake and shaking for the rest of the night. The next morning we ate breakfast together and he left."

◆ ◆ ◆

Surprise — then, courage. My wife, June, was leaving the school where she taught when three teenagers came up behind her, thrust a gun in her back, and demanded money. She simply turned around, put her hand on the gun and turned it over, saying, "You kids don't mean that. Now get out of here." Surprised by her courage, they ran off.

That adds another element: acting with authority. Most people, when they encounter a person of unquestionable authority, automatically defer to it. June's would-be muggers were completely cowed by her firmness. As in all forms of nonviolence, we need to come to terms with our fear of death. We need to be able to send forth love toward potential attackers. But there are situations where neither nonviolence nor violence can avert one's being killed. This is where a strong belief in our unassailable union with the Eternal may be all that we can cling to, in life or in death.

◆ ◆ ◆

That would have been a good place to stop. But there is one more story that is so absolutely brilliant that it deserves to be featured. I don't know who the author or teller is. As best I can recall it, there was an old man who lived next to a school. Every day, when school was out, boys would pass by the porch where the old man was sitting and curse him with every epithet they knew. One day the old geezer called them over and said to them, "Tomorrow when you come by I'll give you a dollar if you'll cuss me out." That was too good a deal to pass up, so they agreed. Next day they came back and cussed him royally. "That's fine," he said, paying up. "Now, tomorrow I'll give you fifty cents each to cuss me out." "Sure," they said, and they did. Next day, "Now I'll give you a quarter to cuss me out." They agreed, looking puzzled. "Now," he said, "I'll give you a penny to cuss me out." "No, way, that's not worth it," they complained and refused to cuss him any longer.

Part Two

TO LOVE
TENDERLY

10

"Contemplation" as the False Self

RICHARD ROHR, O.F.M.

We don't teach meditation to the young monks. They are not ready for it until they stop slamming doors.
— Thich Nhat Hanh to Thomas Merton in 1966

The piercing truth of this statement struck me as a perfect way to communicate the endless disguises and devices of the false self. There is no more clever way for the false self to hide itself than behind the mask of spirituality. And the more mature the spiritual mask looks, the more dangerous it is. Thus things like professional religious roles, honorific titles, special clothing, any disciplined practice or asceticism, all visible shows of piety have always been seen as risky at best by spiritual teachers; Jesus himself warns against them and avoids them personally (see Matt. 6:1–6, 11:18–19, and 23:1–12).

But these ego-masks take a new form in every age. It is easy and even trendy to bash public religious roles, but it is very hard to critique the current movements of "spirituality": specialized forms of prayer, new up-to-date postures and teachers, and especially any form of meditation or contemplation. They can also be used by the unstable ego to give itself identity, self-image, definition, and power.

The human ego will always try to name, categorize, fix, control, and insure all its experiences. For the ego everything is a commodity. It lives inside of self-manufactured boundaries instead of inside the boundaries of the Godself. It lives out of its own superior image instead of mirroring the image of God. With the Western isolated self in a state of immense insecurity today, we are flailing about, searching for any solid identity. "Why not see myself as an enlightened person? Why not read the appropriate authors and attend the appropriate workshops? Why not try on the 'spiritual' persona?" We can thus concoct a quick "salvation," without ever really growing up or "dying" to our false selves at all. A spiritual self-image gives us status, stability, and security. There is no better way to remain unconscious than to baptize and bless form instead of surrendering to substance. I know this because I have done it myself.

Spiritual seeking, when it is done by the false self, might be the biggest problem of all. In the name of seeking God, the ego just pads and protects itself, which is an almost perfect cover for its inherent narcissism. Is it any surprise that America has churches on every corner and yet remains a highly racist, materialistic, militaristic, and superficial culture? We have found the way to feel good about ourselves and to think badly of everybody else that is not like us. Only one thing is more dangerous than the individual ego, and that is the group ego. Religion produces saints and very whole people, but it also produces and protects people with high capacities for delusion and denial. The corruption of the best is always the worst. But let's allow Thomas Merton to say it, in the brilliant way that he always does:

> Suppose that my "poverty" be a secret hunger for spiritual riches: suppose that by pretending to empty myself, pretending to be silent, I am really trying to cajole God into enriching me with some experience — what then? Then everything becomes a distraction. All created things interfere with my quest for some special experience. I must shut them out, or they will tear me apart. What is worse — I myself am a distraction. But, unhappiest thing of all — if my prayer is centered in myself, if it seeks only an enrichment of my own self, my prayer itself will be my greatest potential distraction. Full of my own curiosity, I have eaten of the tree of Knowledge and torn myself away from myself and from God. I am left rich and alone and nothing can assuage my hunger: everything I touch turns into a distraction. (*Thoughts in Solitude*, 93)

Remember that the very word "person" comes from the Latin word for "mask" or for the actor's "part" in a drama. The Judeo-Christian tradition would see all human personhood as a real and organic participation in the *one personhood* that is God. In other words, the human self has no meaning or substance apart from the Selfhood of God. God's personhood is not a mask, but the face behind all masks. We are the masks of God, and we play out God's image in myriad human ways. The immense problem we are facing in a secular society is that we do not know we are the masks of God. We are therefore condemned to creating our own significance, our own legitimation, our own mask and personhood. This makes us — like atoms — inherently unstable. When we do not see our lives as a participation in Another, we are forced to manufacture our own private significance. Contemporary psychology had to create a word for this, and again chose the Latin word for "I," or "ego." It is the atomized self, the small self, the false self, which does not really "exist" at all. In such a state of insecurity, it overdefends itself and overdefines itself. We call this the imperial ego, and it is the basis for all illusion and all evil. It is Adam and Eve trying to survive outside of the Garden, and they can't.

Quite simply, love or charity cannot happen (1) when the self is comparing or differentiating itself from the other (the judging-labeling mind), (2) when the self is trying to dominate over the other (the controlling-punishing mind), or (3) when the self is in competition with the other (the winning-succeeding mind). None of us should assume these demon minds are dead in us until we have been tried and tested in the school of relationships for a long time. In fact, we should assume these are our normal and learned stances. Jesus himself had to face all three in the desert before he could begin his spiritual path.

Right now, contemplation is "in" within many religious and even secular circles. It is a way of being spiritual without any usual accountability, social action, or quality control. It is a way to be religious without being part of a religion. No dues, no priesthood, no commandments, no social grouping, no I-Thou relationship if you don't care for one. It utterly appeals to the Western individualist and introvert, and the ego payoff is major — a very superior self-image: "I am a mediator. I live in serenity above the fray of religious scandals and social concern." There is no system of checks and balance unless I allow it, and no God except the one I experience and decide for. I can do it all in the privacy of my own home and attend conferences and workshops that I judge to be worthy. The small self risks being utterly enthroned. There are no outer reference points of Scripture, society, or symbol to call me out of myself and back to Reality. And remember, "reality is the best ally of God."

A friend, Suzanne Stabile, gave me a lead for this essay when she pointed out to me Abraham Maslow's "hierarchy of needs." As you might remember, he says that one cannot meet higher needs at any level of depth if the lesser needs are not first tended to. One cannot do an "end run" to levels of communion and compassion, for example, when one's basic security and survival needs have not been met. As Jesus put it, when you are "worried about many things," you cannot have faith. When you cannot enjoy the lilies of the field or the sparrows in the sky, don't waste time thinking you can enjoy God. First we must face our block-ing patterns and personality defects, or we will invariably *use* the higher faculties to run from the foundational work. Much of church work, I am afraid, is evangelizing, baptiz-ing, and even ordaining the false self. It is largely a waste of time. We end up trying to be spiritual before we have learned to be human! It is a major problem. Maybe this is why Jesus came to model humanity for us — much more than divinity. Once we get the human part down and "stop slamming doors," we can teach people how to recognize and live from their God center. Up to that point it will almost certainly be a mere self-serving cliché, a phrase, a concocted self-image, frosting on a noncake.

It has been said by many that we are not human beings trying to become spiritual, but we are spiritual beings trying to become human. The first appears to be the unconscious premise of almost all organized religion. It starts on the wrong foot and ends up on the wrong path, which only leads to these kinds of distortions.

"How can I be more holy?" We don't have to make ourselves holy. We already are, and we just don't know it. In Christian terminology it is called the Divine Indwelling or the free gift of the Holy Spirit. That proclamation, and all that proceeds from it, is the essential, foundational, and primary task of all religion. Thus authentic religion is more about subtraction than addition, more letting go of the false self than any attempt at engineering a true self. You can't create what you already have.

The unique character of contemplation in the monotheistic religions is the momentous and life-altering recognition of the Face of the Other. It recognizes and cherishes the gift of the I-Thou relationship that is shown in the midst of silence and emptiness. Here there is not just Someone to love and be loved by, but also Someone to be accountable to *outside myself.* God is personal, and it is a relational universe. In fact our personhood could be seen as precisely that human quality which makes it possible to connect with the personhood of God. We are the same at that point.

Yes, God is Being itself, but also a Being that *is* more me than I am myself. Frankly, this changes everything. God has become a Thou, and not just an energy field. And I have become an I, and not just a statistic. And the path is relationship itself and not just practice, discipline, or holy posture. Authentic contemplation of the Other, through all the necessary stages of personal relationship, calls us beyond our tiny and false selves and into The Self. We become the One we gaze upon. And "the eyes by which we look back at God are the same eyes by which God has first looked at us" (Meister Eckhart). This reciprocal gaze *is* the true self, perfectly given and always waiting to be perfectly received. It is so dear and so precious that it needs no external payoffs whatsoever. The true self is abundantly content.

11

The Formation of the False Self and Coming into the True Self

M. BASIL PENNINGTON, O.C.S.O.

The process that forms in us a sense of self, which unfortunately leads to the creation of a false self when we identify with it, begins in the womb. For the most part the womb is a perfect environment, and the little person therein is quite content and well cared for. It is when this little one is ushered out from this idyllic world of around-the-clock care that he or she begins to experience need. Whether the need is hunger or comfort from the pain of a pinprick, the child has only one way of indicating need: a largely indeterminate cry. A very attentive and loving caregiver can begin to sense the message in the cry or soon enough determine it and attend to it.

It does not take long for newborns to identify the source from which they can hope to obtain the things that are needed: the parents or the parent substitutes. The little ones quickly identify with this source, feel a relative contentment and security when the provider is near at hand, confident that as the needs arise they will be met. A good relationship with this source becomes an instinctual motive. And this relationship opens the way for the parents to fulfill their educative role.

Parents' love is one of the most God-like things in creation. Together with God the parents have brought this little one into being. And like God's, their love is totally gratuitous. The little one has done absolutely nothing to merit it. It is such a beautiful thing, this wholly gratuitous love. The image of the husband of one of my nieces comes to mind. Doug is a big man, tall and well built, an excellent basketball player, a real jock. I can remember vividly, one day shortly after his first daughter was born (they now have three), I came upon Doug, sitting in a chair, holding that little one in his great hand. His whole being was enraptured. Torrents of love poured out from him almost visibly. For me it was a wonderful image of the Divine Love. If a child always received such totally gratuitous, totally affirming love, the child would grow up to be one of the most beautiful persons this world has known.

From Divine Love to the False Self

Unfortunately the scenario often changes. Parents, conscious of their responsibility to educate their child and perhaps, also, investing too much of themselves in the success of this project, feeling they themselves will be judged a success or failure in this regard, begin to trade off on their love for the child to get the child to perform in a certain way: They say to the child — sometimes actually in words but more often in their actions, "Mummy won't love you if you don't...eat your spinach, act like a little lady, be good to your sister," etc. "Daddy won't love you if you don't put your toys away, make a home run in Little League, get a gold star at school."

The message the little ones get through all of this is that they are not lovable in themselves. They are lovable only because of what they do. They have value, they have worth, they are lovable because they perform in an acceptable way.

This sense is reinforced by peers. Who is the popular child? At first it may be more the one who has certain things: the TV game, the sandbox, the bike, the swimming pool...whatever. Later, it will be more and more the one who can do certain things: the good ballplayer, the good dancer, the one who gets good marks in school, etc.

It does not take that long for the message to get through to the developing persons. Their value depends on what they have, what they do, what others — especially significant providers, real or potential — think of them. Others see them this way. And they begin to see themselves this way. This is the construct of the false self. It is made up of what I have, what I do, and what others think of me.

In today's developed societies it is the doing that takes predominance. How often, when we introduce ourselves, do we add what we do: "I am Joe Jones; I am vicepresident at Sperry's." "I am Susan Tam; I teach at the university." And if new acquaintances do not add this attribute to their introduction, we will probably ask them fairly quickly, "What do you do?" This is one of the reasons why it is so difficult for individuals in our culture to retire. For some it is seen to be a death knell, which is, in fact, what it is. For forty years it has been "I am Joe Jones; I am vice-president at Sperry's." Now suddenly it is "I am Joe Jones...." Because individuals so often identify themselves primarily with "doing" — the pivot of the false self — retirement virtually becomes nonexistence, followed by a scramble to create another false self.

Stop for a moment. Ask yourself: how do I introduce myself? How do I want people to see me? Is it made up of what I have, what I do? Who do I say that I am? To myself? To others? Who am I really?

Jesus and the True Self

St. Paul tells us that Christ suffered the things he did in order that he might learn. In the three temptations of Christ we see him learning to say an emphatic "no" to the temptation to create a false self. After forty days of intense fasting, Jesus was a very hungry man. The tempter easily suggested that Jesus might establish himself by doing. It would be easy enough for the man who would later feed five thousand from five loaves to create a tempting meal for himself out of a few stones. But Jesus had a better food. Then how about establishing himself by building esteem? Off to the high point of the temple they went. The courtyards were full of devout worshipers. Surely if he suddenly descended from on high and stood in their midst they would recognize him as the Messiah. But Jesus needed no such acclaim to know who he truly was. Then how about having? What a sense of power, to have all the kingdoms of the world! That would certainly make him something. But this man was poor in spirit. He knew himself in his relation with God. He would not find his identity in what he could do, in what others thought of him, in what he had. He was who he was before God and in God.

This is not the place where most people live. Rather we live in the domain of the false self. And it is not a very happy place to live. Oh, we can distract ourselves up to a point, acquiring ever more, doing ever more, being indispensable (even priests and monks try that), go, go, go. Yet it is a fearful existence, living in this false self — and a perilous one in this competitive world in which we live. We must ever be defensive. And it is a lonely place. We must never let anyone get too close. They might just discover what we so fearfully know: that down beneath all that we have and all that we do, is that little one who is all need and is ever trying to win the approbation of others in the hope that it might ultimately assure us that we are worth something. Jesus said we must die to self. It is precisely this false self that he is talking about — this self which we construct and which in turn imprisons us and makes us serve it in varying degrees of misery. We want to escape the demands it places on us through our own superego and through a society that is wholly dedicated to fostering the values of the false self. But how can we escape? How can we die to the false self, if it is the only self we know? If we die to the false self and we do not know the true self, where are we? The best way to die to the false self is to enter into the practice of a pure prayer, like Centering Prayer.

Every time you are unhappy, just ask yourself, Why am I unhappy? Is it not because I cannot do something I want to do, I do not have something I want to have, or I am concerned about what others will think? It will ultimately be one of these three: The false self is the domain of unhappiness. This is the insight of that Buddhist teaching which tells us to give up all desire. With the realization of the folly to try, as it were, to create ourselves by our doing and having we can begin to take the first steps forward by laughing at ourselves each time we catch ourselves. "Oh, there I go again, trying to make something of myself by this doing, doing, doing." When we laugh at ourselves, we will find a new freedom. I do not have to do to be; I am.

The Way of Centering Prayer

Where we effectively die to this false self is in the practice of a prayer like the Centering Prayer. After all, when we sit down to center, what are we doing? Essentially nothing. Unlike methods of meditation where we do something — watch our breath, use a mantra, etc., in Centering Prayer we simply "be." We use a prayer word, or a sacred word if you will, only in those moments when we realize we have again reverted to doing something: thinking about something, remembering something, feeling something. Then we use our word to return to the simple state of being. Or perhaps more accurately, it is not even being, but allowing God to be in us and express God's being in us, in our being. We are no longer doing anything. Let it be done unto me according to your Word. There is little chance here to build up a false sense of self by doing.

And what do people think of us as we sit there? Most would judge us to be at least a bit off the mark, wasting time, if not a bit crazy. And our false self readily joins with them in this appraisal. "Get up and get going! Do something! Why are you wasting your time? Isn't this all so stupid? Who are you trying to fool?" Etc.

And what do we have when we enter into Centering Prayer? The last thing we are willing to give up is our own thoughts. Take everything else away from me, I know my own mind. The pernicious philosophy that has so formed our times, that of Descartes, has as its bottom line: I think, therefore I am. This is, of course, just the reverse of reality. I am and therefore I think, I dance, I play, I pray. . . . In pure prayer, like Centering Prayer, I give up even my thoughts. I hold on to nothing, to no thing, not even to no-thingness. I claim nothing. And I certainly do not seek to make something of myself for having something.

This is what I do as I enter into the prayer. And I have to do again and again during the prayer, by the use of my prayer word, for I find myself again and again reverting to my thoughts. It may be the things I am thinking about that are grabbing me: things I am doing or things that I have — again the fabric of the false self — or maybe just the cleverness of my own thoughts or my ability to think. The false self is ready to grab on to anything in its gasping attempt to avoid annihilation. And so, in the practice of our prayer, save in those blissful moments when the Divine does indeed embrace us and bring us into our true selves in the Divine Self, we again and again gently use our word to leave all this phoniness behind. Even in this we have to take care that we do not turn the use of the word into a doing. It must simply be a letting go, a surrender to the Divine, who alone creates the true self.

And What Remains?

To die to the false self is challenging indeed — all the more challenging if we do not yet know our true self. If we die to the false self and do not know our true self, where are we? What is the reality?

Some people think of creation as though God made this thing and then tossed it out into space to let it fend for itself. By no means. All that is, is of God. At every moment creation comes forth from the Eternal Creative Love. There is not a moment when the Divine Creative Energy is not fully present to creation, for in such a moment all would simply cease to be.

So the reality is, when we come into being in the womb and come forth from the womb, we are not just some little bundle of absolute need. At the center and heart of our being is the Divine Creative Energy, an Energy that is Love, each moment bringing us forth in love. When we are willing to enter into pure prayer, willing to leave everything behind and go to the center, we open ourselves to the possibility of coming to experience this Divine Presence. True, it is totally within the Divine Discretion and Freedom to decide when and how the Loving God will reveal Godself to us. But the Lord has assured us, "Ask and you shall receive, seek and you shall find." It is with the confidence of faith and the appeal of love that we open ourselves at the center. And in ways beyond the meager limits of our rational faculties we come to know: know the Divine Present, know ourselves in the Divine Creative Love, know everyone else, one with us, in that Creative Love.

Theologically we know by Revelation that we come forth from God in Christ, the crown and center and immediate source of creation: "Through him all things came into being and apart from him nothing came to be. Whatever came to be in him, found life." And we return to God in Christ in that embrace of Love who is Holy Spirit. We cannot really comprehend or grasp this. We have to let Revelation be; we have to let ourselves be grasped by the Realities it expresses. Then we will know them in the love-knowledge that is beyond the rational intellect even illumined by faith. We are in the realm of the Wisdom that comes from the Spirit.

This experience is absolutely literally ineffable. I will fall back on the repeated words of St. Bernard (which used to annoy me when I was beginning on my own journey): "Those who have experienced this know what I am talking about. And those who have not had the experience — have the experience and then you will know."

Once we have had this experience, and even to some extent when we have embraced in faith the reality of this even though we have not yet experienced it, a "transformation" of consciousness takes place within us. The basic and abiding "form" of our consciousness is changed. We no longer identify with the concocted false self, made up of what I do, what I have, and what others think of me. I now know that I am existing within and ever flowing forth from the Divine Creative Energy of the I AM. Here is freedom, here is empowerment, here is life, here is love beyond all telling.

This is the domain of the true self — a place of wonderful freedom, joy, and peace. We begin to enter into the experience of that Christian koan, "I live, now not I, but Christ lives in me." Even as the Father begets the Son in an eternal total self-expression, so does the Creative Energy of the Godhead beget each one of us in Christ, the incarnate Son, the firstborn of creation.

Even when we know our true selves we still have to realize our social role in this world, in the human community, but we will be clear now that this is a role. It is not what makes us but it is the way in which we collaborate with the Divine and our sisters and brothers in making this world and bringing it to its fullness.

But there is something more here. For in finding our true self in God, we find everyone else in God. Indeed, we come to experience our true oneness with all in our common humanity and even more in our oneness in Christ, the head of humanity. We are drawn to enter deeply into the mystery of God's love working in the life of each one of us. There is a union and a communion. We come to love our neighbors in truth as our very selves.

This experience of God and the perception of our true self does not usually happen the first time we center — though God can give one this experience whenever and to whatever extent God wants. It may not happen the fiftieth time or the five-hundredth time. It will happen when God knows we are ready for it. Usually it is a gradual experience. We perceive as it were glimpses of the Divine in the activity of the Spirit, which produces in us the fruits of the Spirit: love, joy, peace, patience, kindness. . . . In our desire for more we should not fail to appreciate this. I have often had people say to me, I have been meditating for so many months or years and nothing is happening; I don't know if I am doing it right, or I don't know if I am meant for contemplative prayer, etc. After we talk a bit they begin to see that, yes, now they are basically more peaceful, happier, more patient. And what certainly is a most precious fruit of the activity of the Spirit within: they have been faithful to their practice. What a tremendous grace it is to have the wisdom to set aside time regularly to respond to our Lord's invitation, "Come to me, all you who labor and are heavily burdened, and I will refresh you." They have become men and women of prayer. That is a tremendous fruit.

12

To Dream and Hope for a Better World

FREDERIKA CARNEY

To our grandchildren: as you move out into a world that will shape you and be shaped by each of you in your own inimitable fashion, I hope you will remember that we all stand on the shoulders of remarkable men and women who built our nation. Their vigor and generosity have created more opportunity for more people than anywhere else in any other era. Yet this might be one of the most emotionally challenging times in history. The physical comforts, advantages, and opportunities are more abundant than ever before, but the signs of deterioration amid the plenitude are startling. There is much that is dysfunctional, out of balance — the immense focus on acquisition and status, the glorification of war, of smart bombs and killing, the greed for power. And now there is an intensified tension of fear, often politically induced but, indeed, a reality. It might be the first time when we are all utterly vulnerable and unprotectable — the rich and the poor alike.

Dennis Kucinich, one of the few in Congress who has spoken out against war and for the need to rethink our direction, said, "Hope is an imminent reality, a reality that is waiting to be called forth. Indeed, one could say we called forth the right to vote for people who were not property owners. We called forth the Emancipation Proclamation. We called forth the right of women to vote. Throughout our country's history, there are moments when change happens and it seems to have happened all at once. But the truth of the matter is it came about because over the many years, people relentlessly pursued their dreams and hopes." In quoting from Shelley's *Prometheus Unbound,* he spoke about "hope creating from its own wreck the thing that it contemplates."

That is our task today: to dream and hope for a better world. The Berlin wall came down and Communism collapsed in Russia without a gunshot because people were sitting around kitchen tables and living rooms, dreaming and hoping, which led to action and change. As old solutions begin to crack and die, new ideas are born and start to bloom. Wherever there is death, there is birth.

In spite of the prevailing currents, I believe that we are living in one of the most exciting periods of transition in all of history. The fact that 15 million people marched for peace around the world is just one of many indications of a global leap in consciousness.

Our challenge is not only to recognize injustice, oppression, propaganda (mind domination), etc. with enough outrage to prompt deep concern and action, but to do so *without* a measure of hatred, disdain, or contempt. Augustine said it sixteen hundred years ago: hate the sin but love the sinner. Jesus said love your enemies. He didn't say don't have enemies! The Dalai Lama has perhaps done more to address this crucial point than anyone else. The Tibetan monks, thousands of whom were despicably tortured, burned alive, and murdered in their monasteries, have expressed and acted with immense compassion for the Chinese who perpetrated these heinous crimes. It is one of the greatest examples of human dignity, forgiveness, courage, and transcendence in all of history.

Admittedly I have a hard time feeling compassion for individuals in our government who are the chief architects of our aggressive, corporate warfare state and its goal of empire. Very few of us have had the training that is required for a compassionate response to those whose behavior we abhor. And though many of the great spiritual teachers and mystics of the past have understood union with all that is and have known that the human race is truly one human family, this is not familiar ground for most of us.

All the myths and most religions have taught love for the "insiders" and distrust, even hatred for the "outsider." In fact, civilization was founded on groups bound together in their fear and distrust of the "outsider." Nothing bonds a group more than a scapegoat or scapegoats upon whom each individual can posit his or her individual hostilities. *Vengeance* in ancient Aramaic was the same word as *justice*. This behavior has been wired into us. But it is changing. We are beginning to think with our hearts.

Leaders will come forth who will lift us to the next level one by one, inch by inch. And like the concentric rings that move out from a stone thrown into a pond, enlightenment will proceed. The sociologists tell us that it takes only about

25 percent of a population to internalize a radical concept, to "get it" and then carry the rest.

My prayer for each of you is that you give your inner voice the silence and attention it needs to grow. It is only here that the real you exists, where you have access to universal wisdom. It is the realm in which you know things that you don't know you know. It is here one is freed from the static of the world and becomes empowered to send and receive with clarity.

As T. S. Eliot said, "... you *are* the music, ... music heard so deeply that is it not heard at all ... and the rest is prayer, observation, discipline, thought and action."

13

And Laugh at Gilded Butterflies
Reflections on Aging

FREDERIKA CARNEY

In our youth we are occupied with planting a flag on the rampart of life. Getting old is so remote that it doesn't even seem a possibility. Death is inconceivable, though we see it around us. Even the Bhagavad-Gita mentions this strange split between our intellectual knowledge and our emotional sense of immortality. It is someone else who will die in the car crash, not me. But as we age a gradual consciousness begins to seep into our psyche. We begin to realize that the hourglass is emptying. The signs of diminished hearing and vision, the creaking and stiffening, the little lumps or heart flutters are all reminders that we must make friends with death.

Almost all societies in the past have honored the wisdom and vision of their elders. But in our tribe we have become *homo economicus,* greedy for achievement and acquisition.

Information has replaced wisdom. Young people are targeted as a large buying market. The elderly are shunned, often neither respected nor admired. The marketplace is the driving force.

It is not an easy time to grow old.

Years ago we met an elderly Japanese gentleman who was a Buddhist. In a moment of social nervousness my husband asked him what he did. He smiled and quietly said, "I have been studying the spirit for the last twenty-five years." The Hindus, also, set aside the last quadrant of life for study, service, and contemplation, in contrast to our status-oriented culture where we want to remain in the driver's seat until the end. The legacy of Nietzsche is that we are the sole authors of our destiny. We forget that we are cocreators and that, indeed, we have a partner — the Holy Spirit. If the value and significance of our life is not given prior to and independent of our performance, then everything will depend on our performance. Everything will depend upon competing, winning.

I keep thinking of how Dante put the great warrior and hero Ulysses in hell because he didn't know how to grow old. He couldn't go into the glorious phase of life where success becomes secondary, where frequently, even regularly, the Divine Self subjugates the ego self.

Will I keep repeating the old pattern, looking for the same achievements, or am I ready for a different journey, one that goes into the desert of humility and contrition, of Love and Forgiveness, into a new language beyond "my" roles, beyond my need to fix situations and relationships?

We are born with a bottomless sense of inadequacy. Augustine named it *original sin*. When we are young we spend a lot of energy countering it, proving ourselves. Old age permits a tolerance through the slow realization that "these are the jokes," this is the "me" that there isn't enough time to reconstruct. Old age offers the space to forgive myself as well as others, to accept myself just as I am, self-deceits and all, to accept our children, our siblings, our friends, just as they are. The process begins with entering a dark wood with steps both timid and bold, holding the paradoxes, absorbing the opposites, remembering that we are part of a dying and rising universe. Like the grain of wheat that first must die in the dark ground, the birth of a new self requires the death of the old. It requires assuming responsibility for my negative choices, contrition, and the releasing of blame. It becomes a vigil — catching myself in the moments of feeling virtuous and recognizing these old ego games, realizing that if I ask God for forgiveness and yet cannot forgive myself, this is another ego trick in the form of pride, which assumes I should be better, more evolved. It is a never-ending process of releasing.

Shakespeare addresses "letting go" in some of the most beautiful lines in the English language when King Lear speaks to his daughter Cordelia. She wants to confront the wicked sisters. " . . . No, no, come, let's away to prison: We two alone will sing like birds i' the cage, . . . we'll live and pray and sing and tell old tales and laugh at gilded butterflies . . . and take upon us the mystery of things as if we were God's spies." Lear has totally released not only his power but his attachment to his old world. The verbs tell us how to live: listen, pray, sing, laugh. And in the end "wear out" the mobs, the politicians, the grasping rulers who are caught up in the "ebb and flow" of the moon.

103

Lear is filled with joy that comes through Love, not the love that is possession or neediness or desire, but transcendent Love that is rooted in forgiveness — forgiveness not only of one's self but of humanity. Lear kneels down for Cordelia's pardon and blessing, transformed by his losses.

To "take upon us the mystery of things" is to move into the Mysterium Tremendum, which is God, a God of forgiveness, a God of mercy, who embraces all the paradoxes of life. Lear has transcended the hatred of his daughters who imprisoned him. He has exchanged his anger for forgiveness. And in this transformation he is at *union with all that is.* He is connected to every sentient and nonsentient being. He is filled with joy that moves in him like tiny grains of yeast permeating and lifting the dough.

How do we cultivate the humility that King Lear discovered and reach the vulnerable state that becomes transcendent? All the great world masters teach us that humility is the beginning. Written on Apollo's temple at Delphi is "Know thyself." For the Greeks this meant to know you are not immortal, that you are a limited, flawed creature. That is where you start, and when you forget it, you move into hubris.

For me, the Catch-22 has always been that in order to assume true humility through the acceptance of all of our flaws, one must first have spiritual confidence. I don't think it is possible to be humble without knowing that we are secure. For Christians we find safety in God's love. Our continuity is restored through prayer. We live our lives balancing the fact that we are made in the divine image of God, Imago Dei, and in the same breath that we are flawed, limited, disconnected souls. Often we forget the first part of the equation and are bowed down by the second. As Thomas Merton said, "If we knew how much God loved us, there would be no sin." We wouldn't have to spend most of our life proving that we are okay. There would be nothing to win; we are already there, in the shadow of God's boundless grace. We neglect this delicate balance at our own peril: we are neither wholly divine nor wholly inadequate. We are always both.

How do we "break the staff and drown the book" as Shakespeare's Prospero does in his final letting go? My husband is an author who is still engaged with his writing. Most publishers are not interested in an eighty-year-old without a broad following. At times he wants to give up; but expressing himself with words is a significant part of who he is. He keeps on going, sometimes with success and often not. The answer is to purify his motive. Do it for God, and to the measure that he puts aside his hope for recognition or financial success, the burden is lifted. Of course, the old longings don't disappear, but the edge is gone, and more and more often he is able to let go of results. A visible sweetness grows in him, a gratitude for what he has. There is nothing to complete, nothing to finish, just the gratitude and delight that comes from contributing his share.

Often I have wished for an Angelus, a bell tolled to prompt us into a remembrance of God. If a moment at dawn could be repeated at noon and in the evening as faithfully as the Angelus in the Middle Ages, when every knee dropped to the ground, every head bowed, and we let go of our agendas for a few seconds and said our communal prayer, I think we would be a very different people.

Old age allows time for a faithful prayer life that may have been intermittent in the past. My husband had never said so much as a decade of the rosary since his childhood when the nuns prepared him for First Communion. After a dream of the Blessed Mother he started saying the rosary at bedtime. When I'm out on my bicycle with the dogs, lines from the Psalms come to mind: "This is the day the Lord has made, Let us rejoice and be glad" (Ps. 118). "The Lord is my light,... whom shall I fear?" (Ps. 27). One of my favorite prayers is one that David Hawkins, M.D., Ph.D., says: sit with your arms slightly raised and hands held up in order to radiate out that which you would give to humanity. You ask of the world what it needs and you become a channel for God's mercy and guidance. You think of kindness and it will move through you undiffused.

It is very hard when we are young to realize that we are superfluous — no more than a teardrop in the ocean, a speck in the cosmos. Years ago I heard a description of an old couple sitting on a porch; they weren't holding hands or speaking but were joined in an aura of silence and devotion, bound by their mutual faith in the goodness of life. I remember wondering if I would ever experience such moments. For me it took many struggles, many awakenings to release the anguished eye of desire, to move beyond distractions into a deep sense of kinship with all things. Serenity comes after decades of surrender to one another, to all the little flaws and rancor. There are times when Otis and I are overwhelmed by gratitude and the harmony of our life. These are the crowning gifts of old age.

14

My Integration

ROBIN CHISHOLM

Whenever I am troubled I head for the beach. Fortunately I live in Adelaide, South Australia, which has beautiful beaches within twenty miles of downtown. A broken marriage, a struggling business, and raising three adolescent children just got to be too much for me one day about eighteen months ago. So the beach was calling! Four days of retreat in a holiday shack on a secluded beach led to an unfamiliar need to express my thoughts and emotions. I've always thought of myself as a serious, action type, with little time for poetry and such reflective pastimes. However, sitting on that beach — listening and watching the rocks and waves — moved me to write this poem. As I sat there that fine sunny winter's morning, I became the rocks and waves. The troubles didn't go away, but I found new strength to handle them.

♦ ♦ ♦

Am I a rock, proud against the waves' relentless clock
Am I a rock, defiant, silent, amid the boiling bubbles
Am I a rock mocking the waves in their froth and
    struggles
Am I a rock so still and grey,
to taunt the waves through night and day?

The rock does not give, it does not take
It mocks the waves and the cries they make
It has no light or life it seems,
its steadfast form is its only means.

Am I the waves who frolic and play
constant each morning, night and day
Am I the waves, no light of their own,
but reflecting the sky as they cry and groan
Am I the waves with laughter loud
who beat upon those rocks so proud
Am I the waves mighty and strong
Will they win and prove who's wrong?

The waves would have the rock shaped round
smooth and in submission found
and over the centuries with eons past
who will win the victory last?

Yet rock and wave though different be
their fight and struggle seem to me
a life united, spirit fast
to live and be in harmony.

I am the rock and waves divergent still
but in union one day a child to thrill

To be one day a beach of sand
as if it all before was planned
Gentle and soft, so finely made
that children can in safety wade.

Years of struggle, conflict, pain,
in union now all wholeness gain
Once loud and boisterous proud and grey
new life is found in prayer and play.

◆ ◆ ◆

15

Thoughts on Psalm 23

PAULA D'ARCY

THE LORD ... The one who holds everything in being, and whose hand sweeps across the void, and there is life. How often have I been touched with the sweep of that hand, and not recognized either the hand or its love when I first felt the touch?

I'm twenty-seven years old. It was a terrible accident. Everything I love is broken.

I'm scared.

And the doctor walks into my hospital room and says, "I'm sorry, Paula. I'm so sorry. They did everything they could, but your husband and child will not live."

And deep inside of me there is a scream that has no sound.

LORD, YOU ARE MY SHEPHERD ... And I am asking, how will I go on? How will I care for the child with whom I am pregnant? All I see is the dark. All I hear is stillness. Then, from the mysterious deep comes a small wave of knowing. This is what I know:

I SHALL NOT WANT. How do I know this? My life is in pieces, but I shall not want. And not the words but the truth they bear allows me to sit in my chair as they lower the two coffins into the earth.

And I stay sane.

God is not an object for study. God is the subject. And without anyone knowing, I walk into the sanctuary of the shepherd, and I watch the burial from there. There was NO EVIL TO FEAR. Nothing could harm me.

He was with me.

One cannot learn about prayer without praying. I pray. I pray as if the sense of my life depends upon the answers I will hear. It does.

HE MAKES ME LIE DOWN IN GREEN PASTURES. HE LEADS ME BESIDE THE STILL WATERS. "Rest first" is what I hear. "Rest" is the first response to my prayer. This will take time.

HE GUIDES ME. I am so tired. I sleep in his valley.

And then, the first wave hits. The force of the grief finally finds me. Now I feel it.

THE VALLEY OF THE SHADOW OF DEATH. Now I do not see or recognize any ROD or STAFF. The pain is winning. The pain is winning. And there is no clarity that will help me now. There is no response. There is darkness.

TRUST. The smallest voice utters that sound. TRUST. Is this the voice that is true? It is hard to know, amid the thunder of my circumstances. TRUST. IF YOU WOULD

ONLY TRUST . . . WAIT OUT THE STORM. YOU DO NOT HAVE TO SEE IN THE DARK. I DO.

I want it to be easier. I do not want to take responsibility for my life. And the voice in the valley responds: IF YOU WILL EVER AWAKEN,

YOU MUST TRUST, EVEN IF PAIN IS YOUR TEACHER. Then he PREPARES A TABLE BEFORE ME. SIT DOWN. But I can't. The drunk driver who killed my family is at that table too. I can't. This is not the way out.

SIT DOWN. How could he do this? Why does he ask this of me?

DO YOU WANT TO WAKE UP BEFORE YOU DIE? BE CAREFUL WHAT YOU DECIDE. TRUST IN THE DARK-NESS, PAULA. SIT AT THE TABLE SO YOU WILL BEGIN TO GROW. FACE YOUR EGO. HERE. IN THE DARK, CLING TO ME.

REACH OUT FOR ME. Oh so reluctantly I sit down. I do not want to forgive. My ego is so strong and righteous. But this shepherd who is love will take me no further until I love. I have stopped us. It's up to me. The luxury is over: speaking negatively of my enemy. Thinking of him with judgment and disdain. There can only be one God in a person's life.

I SIT DOWN AT YOUR TABLE. I forgive the man. I do not condone what was done: I do not have to. But I give up judging his soul. Inside of me, I let the judg-ment go. I am surprised . . . this is a choice, not a feeling. And my eyes begin to open. I see my arrogance and my entitlement. Who have I been? I weep. I was entitled to nothing. Everything has been a gift.

AND I AM GIVEN A TABLE IN A COURTROOM. And the gift, without words, of looking deeply into my enemy's eyes. I meet him face to face. But I hardly see him. I see me, and I see the smallest glimpse...a fragment...of the love which fills the universe. And in the darkness, there is brilliant light. And pouring down my cheeks is the OIL. MY CUP OVERFLOWS. AND GOODNESS AND MERCY REVEAL THEMSELVES TO ME.

And there is nothing else I want.

16

The Duty of Confrontation

THOMAS KEATING

If your brother sins [against you], go and tell him his fault between you and him alone. If he listens to you, you have won over your brother. If he does not listen, take one or two others along with you, so that "every fact may be established on the testimony of two or three witnesses." If he refuses to listen to them, tell the church. If he refuses to listen even to the church, then treat him as you would a Gentile or a tax collector. (Matt. 18:15–17)

 The duty of confrontation is a hard one. According to this text, if you see people doing something seriously wrong, there is an obligation, given certain norms of prudence, to bring this fault to their attention so that they do not disintegrate into more and more self-destructive behavior. Just how far this applies to us depends on our vocation. There seems to be a prophetic role in which one is sent by God to call leaders or other people to order. There have been some classical examples in history of people who under the inspiration of the Spirit confronted highly placed people with their faults. We only have to think of John the Baptist, who lost his head, or Thomas More, who complained about the conduct of Henry VIII in similar circumstances and also found himself headless. Certain hazards surround the prophetic role. Hence it is just as well to make sure that we are really sent before we confront the lions in their dens. All of us, however, have to face the duty to correct someone once in a while.

Dealing with teenagers is a constant concern for parents. There is anxiety over whether children are getting into bad company, experimenting with drugs, or exploring conduct that is not suitable for teenagers. At a certain point you may have enough indication of trouble to say, "I must confront this child."

Confrontation never works if it comes out of a feeling of anger. Hence, it is important to choose a suitable time and place and to consider what the other person's situation is so that you have the maximum chance of speaking to that person's heart.

Some people are temperamentally inclined to confront people; nothing gives them greater pleasure. If correction comes from the enjoyment of confrontation, it is not going to get anywhere. Others cannot bring themselves to confront anyone because of shyness or timidity that does not want to rock the boat and inclines them to sweep all kinds of garbage under the rug; the dirt comes out anyway and makes a terrible mess. If they had confronted the problem promptly and out of love, they might have done a great service to someone they love or whom they have a responsibility to correct.

The Lord indicates that if you have tried to correct and have not succeeded, you have fulfilled your duty and no more is expected of you other than to go on praying. He suggests a way of handling difficulties in a community when things are not going well with some of the members: pull them aside and confront them. This is called fraternal correction. If that does not work, you bring in a few prudent persons to discuss the matter; and if that does not work, you bring in the community as a whole. If all these efforts fail, you have completed your duty and now you can treat the offender like tax collectors, whom everybody avoids. You still love the person, but the duty of trying to correct him or her has gone as far as it can go.

Love alone can change people. This is the great confrontation that no one can resist. It offers others space in which to change no matter what they do. Our ill-conceived efforts, especially if they arise from personal annoyance or because the conduct of others might cause us embarrassment, will accomplish nothing. The offenders will sense that the confrontation is not coming from a genuine concern for them and will mobilize their defenses. By showing love no matter what happens, we provide them with a milieu in which they can experience the possibility of changing. This is to imitate God's compassion toward us. He is constantly trying to correct us but never with vindictiveness. When he corrects us, he never pursues us like the Furies of Greek mythology. He simply keeps inviting us to let go of conduct that is self-destructive and to come back to his love. Whenever there is something to be corrected, he indicates that if we amend, we will enjoy complete forgiveness. The only confrontation that leads to correction is to accept whomever we are trying to help just as they are.

Here is a true story about a psychiatric nurse who was told the lurid history of a certain patient who had just entered the hospital. This man had committed a terrible crime. It was so terrible that he never wanted it known. He had completed his long prison sentence and had come to the hospital in a dying condition. He could not believe that God could forgive his crime; hence, he resisted any form of reconciliation. The chaplain tried to persuade him to trust God. He refused. Any thought of reconciliation awakened his self-hatred. It was more painful for him to think of forgiveness than to feel his self-hatred.

The psychiatric nurse showed him every courtesy. She tucked him in at night, provided him with little favors like flowers, remembered his birthday, asked about his family, and wrote him notes on her day off. Because his illness was prolonged, she developed a friendship with him.

Near the end, his closest friend came to see him and urged him to be reconciled with God. "Please don't mention it!" the dying man ordered. "God couldn't possibly forgive me for what I have done."

His friend kept urging, "God is good! He loves you. You can trust him." But nothing he said could penetrate the sick man's defenses. Finally the friend said in desperation, "Think how much love the nurse shows you. Couldn't God do the same?"

The sick man acknowledged how grateful he was to the nurse who had shown him so much love, but he added, "If she knew what I have done, she too would reject me."

His friend replied, "I must make a confession to you. When you first entered the hospital, I confided to her the entire story of your crime in every detail."

The dying man looked at him in stunned astonishment. His defenses dissolved and his eyes filled with tears. "If she could love me," he murmured, "knowing all that I have done, it must be true. God too can love me."

This nurse ministered the sacrament of reconciliation not ritually but actually. She communicated in her very person God's forgiveness and compassion. The sacrament of reconciliation was unacceptable to the man, but God came to him in a person who was able to manifest God's love for him in a concrete way. This is the ultimate confrontation, which is not so much a confrontation as the transmission of divine love.

Part Three

TO WALK HUMBLY
WITH YOUR GOD

17

A Passage through India

RICHARD ROHR, O.F.M.

 It seems that much of my life in recent years has become a sort of cross-cultural "shuttle service": taking some of the pastoral wisdom that we have had time to learn in North America to the communities of Africa, Asia, and Latin America — and bringing back the prophetic wisdom that we often need in our fearful and ailing culture.

I recently returned from a three-week preaching and teaching stint in Calcutta and Bombay at the initial invitation of the archbishop of Calcutta, Henry D'Souza. I was to give retreats to his priests, religious, and lay leaders. He also asked me to spend time with the Missionaries of Charity during their time of transition following the death of Mother Teresa. A month before I left, several lay leaders in Bombay asked me to spend time with them.

I don't know how God orchestrates such symphonies with our lives as God did with me on this trip, especially when we are largely unconscious and unready instruments. It seems that God calls us, uses us, and transforms us, often in spite of ourselves. I have come to call it the Great Mercy.

I began with a six-day retreat for the diocesan clergy of Calcutta. When not working with the priests, I spent as much time as possible at my window or on the streets nearby — feasting my eyes on a world utterly different from my own. Calcutta is the most densely populated city in the world. Not just 9–10 million people, but 9–10 million in a very crowded area. Immediately I was struck by the politeness and easy smiles of almost everybody with whom I made contact. Having just flown from "Catholic" Rome, where you had to watch every minute for pickpockets and purse snatchers, it seemed so respectful to have these Hindus and Muslims hold out their hands — and *ask.*

Maybe this is why Francis and the Buddha wanted their followers to be "mendicants." Begging seemed to create an ambiance of respectful connection, vulnerability, and utter honesty: We are in this human thing together. We do not need to be afraid of one another, but we *do* need to reveal our "nakedness" and neediness to one another. That was my first lesson in this ancient culture: there appeared to be a much finer line between ego and shadow in India. Ego and shadow were not as separate and defended, but somehow seemed to be working up front and together. When ego and shadow are a little kinder to one another, it is a humble spirit that is released.

As the days advanced and I moved beyond superficial contact with the priests and people, I sensed something more. There is something very solid and strong in this culture. Despite the usual personality quirks and problems that all humans have, there was something more reliable and less whimsical here. India's people seemed immensely more patient than we Westerners are and have a much higher tolerance for discomfort and not getting their own way. There was not the quick and superficial laughter that we hear so much; in fact, you could say that most people were quite serious. It was not simply introversion that I was experiencing through them but a new kind of depth.

One woman from Bombay summed it up best when she told me, "In America you know everything about personality but almost nothing about essence. Here in India we know much about essence and hardly bother with personality." Then she asked me to teach the Enneagram in a country where I least expected to teach it. They did not need my meanderings on social justice or any North American encouragements toward simple living — surely their faith in Jesus seemed much deeper than mine. But the humble Indian church recognized that many good church projects unraveled because good and grounded people could still hurt and misunderstand one another. Again the prophetic met the pastoral. East met West. "The eye cannot say to the hand, 'I do not need you'" (1 Cor. 12:21). We *really are* One, most especially when we "defer" to one another and receive the Always Greater Mystery.

I spent three days immersed in the life, spirit, and ministries of Mother Teresa's community — the Missionaries of Charity — exactly a year after her death. The major sessions took place right next to her tomb, or in the large chapel immediately above. We ended on October 1, the feast of her patron, St. Thérèse. All the four hundred plus local candidates, novices, and professed return for this day. The brothers and many of the lay volunteers also joined us for a full day of teaching, praying, and celebrating in the manner of the poor. It is probably the closest I will ever get to what those first idyllic days must have been like for the early Franciscans: utter joy in Jesus and his Gospel, poverty that is almost embarrassing but beautiful, unquestioned belief in what your life means and in what you are doing. It was like meeting a different species of human being!

Finally I had met a "conservative" yet fully contemporary form of religious life that I could fully trust. The sisters were not rigid women, but simple devoted women. These were not people needing security, answers, and order, as we see in most traditionalist movements in the West, but in fact people who were willing to live without security, with very few answers to their questions of mind and heart, and amid almost total *disorder.* All in union — hour by hour — with God. This was that amazing and rare combination of utter groundedness and constant risk-taking that always characterizes the true Gospel. Categories of "liberal" and "conservative" were meaningless here.

These women wasted no time in fixing, controlling, or even needing to understand what is wrong with others. Instead they put all of their time and energy into letting God change *them.* From that transformed place, they serve and carry the pain of the world, which they are convinced is the pain of God. This is the synthesis on a communal level that I have been waiting for. I have met it among many individuals, but hardly ever in public and social form.

I do not believe their lifestyle answers all questions; I do not believe they have all charisms; I do not believe they are necessarily holier than many other Christians I have met. But there is a radical and utterly clear gift of God that is being revealed through them today. I even dared to ask one of the leaders about one of the most common criticisms of Mother Teresa: "Why did Mother not speak out against social injustice? Why did she not point out the evil systems and evil people that are chewing up the poor? Why did she not risk some of her moral 'capital' to call the world, and even the church, to much-needed reform?"

The answer was calm, immediate, and firsthand. Mother Teresa felt that if she took sides, or played the firebrand, that she could not be what Jesus had told her to be — *love to and for all.* She told them that if she started correcting and pointing out "sinners" she could no longer be an instrument of love and reconciliation for them. Humiliated and defensive people do not change. Like her patron Thérèse of Lisieux, "her vocation in the church was to *be love.*" And like Gandhi, that other great reformer in India in the twentieth century, she knew that her primary message had to be *her life itself,* not words or arguments or accusations. She had found that "third something" that is always beyond the calculating and dualistic mind.

Could this not be the essential folly of the cross? Could this not be the nondualistic mind that we are searching for in contemplative prayer? Might this in fact, be the reconciliation of the "two into one . . . the mystery hidden for ages in God" that Ephesians (2:15–3:9) speaks of so hopefully? Is this not the ultimate nonviolent life that we are searching for? In Mother Teresa's community the only "violence" seems to be toward the self — and not toward anybody else. In other words, I let God change *me* instead of first trying to change others. This is radical reform. Mother Teresa neither played the victim nor created victims, but *like Jesus, she became the free and forgiving victim who carried the two sides of humanity inside of herself — until it trans-formed her and made her useable for God.* I know of no other way out of our present and universal dilemma. Yet it has been the Gospel since the beginning.

In India I felt that there was no way to avoid the human dilemma through the usual means of mental gym-nastics, political posturing, or projection of the shadow elsewhere. It is right there, glaring, obvious, overwhelm-ing, and tragic. One either carries it or goes crazy. It is no surprise to me now that the Indian culture was the matrix for both Gandhi and Mother Teresa. Only this many-thousand-year-old culture, the home of the world's oldest religions, has the depth to rediscover the nonviolent teach-ing of Jesus and the Great Compassion of God. Neither Gandhi nor Teresa looked for winners and losers, neither led us out of the human dilemma and "solved" our prob-lems in any way. But just like Jesus, they *led us directly into the human dilemma and agreed to carry it.* These are the true "sons and daughters of God"!

I was struck by this recently as I read the first reading for the feast of my Father, St. Francis. The conclusion of Paul's letter to the Galatians is always used for his feast because it speaks of "bearing the brand marks of Jesus on my body" (6:17) in reference to the stigmata that Francis received in 1224. Yet it seems to contrast this true transformation into the image of Jesus with the merely external symbols and rituals whereby we seek to validate ourselves: "It matters not whether one is circumcised or not [read "baptized," "churched," "morally purified," etc.], *but only that one be created anew"* (6:15).

126

What I saw in both the Missionaries of Charity and many of the Catholics of India was the absolute necessity of being "created anew." Religion in India has to be about transformation, about "being conformed unto the pattern of his death and thereby knowing the power of his resurrection" (Phil. 3:10). There is no time for dressing up and playing church. There is no time or energy for liberal/conservative squabbles, or infighting about who is more orthodox or moral. The "brand marks" of the crucifixion of God are everywhere, and you either agree to carry them with Jesus, or religion remains mere theater and disguised self-interest. In simple words, it is much harder to fake it in India.

So I return to New Mexico profoundly blessed and, I must admit, frightened by the glaring truth that I met in India. I have come to see that our suffering is a momentary and privileged participation in the eternal suffering of God. Christianity was not meant to be a "salvation scheme" creating spiritual country clubs for the elite, but much more *a vocation to share the fate of God for the life of the world.* Christianity is an invitation to be useable for God by walking through the fire of death and resurrection with Jesus. I found myself talking this way as I addressed the Missionaries of Charity. And as so often happens in my life, it was the crowd in front of me that pulled the words out of me. Because they lived it, I could finally see it and say it.

I have been invited back to India to teach every couple of years, and I don't know how I can do that. Yet I know if it is God's will, it will happen. I was amazed that our years of experience at New Jerusalem Community in Cincinnati, our charismatic experience, my Franciscan background, and the integrative concerns of the Center for Action and Contemplation were all very helpful in Calcutta, India! I would never have believed it. Just as all human seeing is stereoscopic (two eyes seeing two different things but our mind making them into one image), maybe East and West, mind and spirit, male and female, body and soul, liberal and conservative are all the split dualisms that Christ has come to overcome. But we must *pay the price for their overcoming* just as he did. That is our Christian vocation. There is nothing elitist or triumphalistic here — just the following of Jesus.

This preacher has spent much of his life talking *about* Jesus. My passage through India has taught me, once and for all, that it is much more important to *be* Jesus — then God can do what God wants. Finally we are not in control, and God is. It has almost nothing to do with worthiness, and almost everything to do with saying "yes" to a call that is our deepest and truest self.

18

A Clandestine Christian

RICHARD ROHR, O.F.M.

And this life, exempt from public haunt,
Finds tongues in trees, books in running brooks,
sermons in stones, and good in everything.

— William Shakespeare, *As You Like It*

 I would like to share with you a few of my journal entries from the recent hermitage that might communicate what I am trying to say in this essay. This short poem I called "Bearing the Mystery":

An excess of life.
Of ideas, of hopes,
Of memories, of friendship.
Of suffering, of youth.

I cannot live long
enough (Each day digesting deep impressions of
Who-You-Are, and who-I-am).

An excess of death,
Of absurdity, of despair.

Of memories, of betrayal.
Of beauty, of old age.

I cannot die quick
enough (nothing inside of me or outside of me
is as bad as my rejection of it).

So I will live them both
And
Die them both
now

"Through Him, with Him, and in Him,"
for the mystery is too heavy to carry alone.

Five years ago I wrote, "There is a rhythm between her-mitage and community that might be even more basic than the classic tension called action and contemplation. One is the school; the other is the lesson." At that time I began living in Franciscan community where I have lived ever since. My first eight years in New Mexico were in a little "her-mitage" in downtown Albuquerque. Both situations have been times of both trial and grace, solitude and social engagement; both were good because of the rhythm itself. I have always learned best, it seems, by contrast and conflict. It is the only way I come to any kind of consciousness or communion. This I know with even deeper conviction five years later: action is the ongoing good and needed school, but the concluding lesson is always a contemplative seeing and being.

Now the opportunity arrives to live again in a small cottage on the grounds of Holy Family Parish next door to the Center for Action and Contemplation. I have already begun to create a prayer garden south and west of the cottage, which one friend has dubbed "the Garden of Eden." (I hope also to build a labyrinth for spiritual walking.) So I might just call this little residence "East of Eden"! As you remember, God sent Cain, with a protective mark, to live "in the land of Nod, east of Eden" (Gen. 4:16). This will be my little hermitage for now — where I hope to follow a stricter regimen of silence, study, prayer, writing, correspondence, and just enough public speaking to pay my rent and pass on some of the fruits of contemplation.

I, like Cain, will trust in God's "protective mark" as I try to do what I have to do. The soul learns best not in security and prefab explanations, but in wandering or being led to places (Nod means "wanderer") where only God is in control. For me, this is "clandestine Christianity," and the only form today that is "clean" enough (without so much agenda) to get me back to the core experience. I have to try it, and maybe it will give others courage too. Otherwise, we will try to solve all our institutional issues from a smaller and smaller inner experience, and with a too often narrow and churchy vocabulary. There has to be something more than "loyalty tests" to prove that you belong to the right group. Loyalty language just isn't big enough for the great mystery of God in Christ.

We have begun a weekly scripture class here on the parish grounds which is very well attended. Luke's Gospel is so much more fascinating when you can take the time to go through the entire text, chapter by chapter, week by week. I plan on teaching whenever I am in town, probably alternating between a book from the Hebrew scriptures and another from the Christian. It also keeps me rooted here at home and with the Center, as I spend less time on the road.

I figure that very few people have had the privilege of having so much of their thought in book and tape form. I have to assume that most of what I have to say has already been said, and I do not need to personally keep gathering frequent-flyer miles! Please pray that I can now *live the life of union with God* that I have talked about to others. All we can really give the world is *who we are*. It is our only truth, our deepest justice, and still the most radical witness that we can share with active and activist people who come to our Center. In my experience, transformed people transform others.

The art form now is how to live just east of Holy Family Parish (where I still serve as substitute priest) and so close to the Center for Action and Contemplation — and not get caught up in the social whirlwind that we call life. There has to be some degree of withdrawal from the revolving hall of mirrors in order to find oneself primarily mirrored by God. Again, this is an urgent need, not just for me personally, but also for a culture that seems lost in monthly media dramas, projections, and conversations that merely fill up the time and temporarily assuage the loneliness. We feel socially contagious today, and no one is benefiting from it: "Sound and fury, signifying nothing." We tend to mirror group feelings instead of knowing who we really are.

We thought that if we stopped believing in God we would be free from belief. But instead we believe in *everything!* Conspiracy theories, medical treatments, fun-damentalism from anywhere except Christianity, power in stars and plants, and crystals, apparitions, and dogmatism seem to be everywhere.

Knowing that this will make me sound like an old curmudgeon to some folks, I still feel that our culture and frankly much of our peace and justice work is dominated by very fragile egos, superficial intellectual and emotional lives, knee-jerk reactions that are often politically correct but nowhere close to the Gospel. As I wrote in my hermitage journal, "the self that begins the journey is not the self that arrives at the Gospel. The self that begins is the self that we *think* ourselves to be, the superior self we want to be. This is the self that dies along the way — until 'no one' is left. This is the true self that all Great Religion talks about, *the self bigger than death yet born of death,* a different self than the private I, a self transformed by God and transformed in God."

This paschal journey is the most radical and true thing that the Center can offer the world, the individual, and the work of activists. Those born of such a death will be the deepest agents of peace and justice, as opposed to the good folks who are just current with the recent spin on things. I am finding that our unique Christian path of transformation is indeed much narrower than I once imagined. It demands death, the death of the small self. How will we ever make that attractive or popular?

If the Center is to offer anything true to the world, if I am to dare to think I have something to say that will last, it has to come from a place of *true union,* and the medium has to be the same as the message. It has become more and more apparent to us that very few places are seeking the precise Gospel integration for social change that we are seeking here at the Center. The true synthesis of action and contemplation is still "the greatest vocation," according to Thomas Aquinas, and for me, the ultimate art and discipline. Pray that we can all do it well — for the sake of the world!

I am already forgetting the only thing that the silence has taught me: *our lives are useable for God. We need not be effective, but only transparent and vulnerable.* God takes it all from there, and there is not much point in comparing who is better, right, higher or lower, or supposedly saved. We are all partial images slowly coming into focus, to the degree we allow and filter the Light and Love of God.

Let me end this attempt at a self-explanation with a quote from a Muslim mystic that I discovered while in hermitage. There it delighted me for days on end, yet now, back in the flurry of images and emotions, I block this simple Light and this always sweet sadness: "God sighs to become known in us. God is delivered from solitude by the people in whom God reveals himself. The sorrow of the unknown God is softened through and in us" (Ibn al-Arabi, 1165–1240).

That's enough work for all of our remaining years. All we can be is transparent and vulnerable. Our authority will be the authority of those who have passed through — and come out on the other side — dead *and* alive.

19

Learning to Be Human

JUSTINE BUISSON

 Why did God choose to enter human history? As Christians, we believe it was to save us, to show us the way to Life. This awesome conjunction of divine and human, this intersection that took place two thousand years ago in Judea, and keeps repeating everywhere — what reassurance that God is with us! And what a reminder that we are invited to continue the Incarnation by becoming the men and women God desires us to be.

In our society today, we see children being hurt in unimaginable ways, women living in terror of their men, young people flinging themselves into destruction through addictions and violence, our fellow citizens in a mad scramble for quick riches, pleasure kicks, entertainment, escape from the reality of life. Others have no lives at all, their human potential not even given a chance.

Such a terrible waste! We want to take the blunderers by the hand and say, "Look, you are supposed to be human!" Isn't this the reason Christ came, and keeps coming — to teach us *how to be human*? The miracle is not only that

God entered our condition — enmeshed in nature, subject to suffering — but that we too might come to reflect the divine intention, share in the mystery of God.

A medieval Muslim mystic, Ibn al-Arabi, wrote, "God is a mystery in his own eyes." What an arresting thought! Artists know this; they create in order to understand. Think with what delirium star systems were flung out, suns set on fire, planets given a home. Think of the long, patient nurturing of sea life, plant life, animal evolution on earth. How God must have enjoyed experimenting with creation: permitting it the freedom of little trials and errors, small achievements, sudden leaps of success. And then the creatures who would image God, who in some inexplicable way could *know* God.

"But wait, they don't have it right. Let me show them what I mean." Even Jesus must have learned slowly what being human means and found it difficult. There was so much confusion in people's minds, so much healing required. To save us from spiritual blindness, he healed the blind. He denounced the priests who had built such a complicated, burdensome structure out of the Mosaic Law. He stood on the outskirts of society, took his place among the wounded, the wretched. Just as Yahweh had taken sides with the Hebrews against Pharaoh, Jesus took sides — with sinners and lepers against the righteous who condemned and shunned them. He tipped the balance of power of the status quo. Jesus demonstrated that being human means caring for, being part of. This is what he taught by example: to reach the divine you must pass through the human, become human yourself.

We are still so far from being the human beings God intends. Did it surprise God that we took a wrong turn away from Eden, where we were friends with God, and lost our way? Or could it be that the Creator left this loophole for us to close? To show that the new heaven and the new earth will not be accomplished without us? Is it possible that God needs our hands and hearts here and now? There are once-revered but distorted structures crumbling all around us. It depends on Christ's people to rebuild them not with stones and rules but with the common good in mind. Other structures are mushrooming like cancer cells, feeding off the weak and the innocent. Some people, like Dorothy Day, decide to stand outside these structures, to live among and minister to the poor. Others refuse to participate in the societal sin of militarism and laws directed against the poor. Some fight greed and indifference by trying to persuade their neighbors and legislators to protect the air, the water, the habitats of our brothers and sisters, the animals.

For all of us, the first step is to become conscious of the evil of our time, to look it in the eye and call it by its real name. Will we be uncomfortable, misunderstood, decried? Certainly, but didn't Jesus call us blessed in advance for standing up for what is right and naming what is wrong? In the morass of evil around us, we need to keep faith with the great mystery trying to understand itself — through us. This, I think, is what it means to be human and to show others that they are called to be human too, as children of God.

20

Sustainability and Spirituality

JOHN E. CARROLL

 "Sustainability" is an all-too-common word describing a condition that these days hardly exists. Indeed, the extremely common usage of the word may be symptomatic of a deeper realization that the condition of sustainability, which most people would posit as both necessary and good, is virtually nonexistent. In fact, almost all usage of the word "sustainability," whether by institutions or individuals, refers to a superficial and cosmetic form of sustainability which is both inaccurate and dishonest. Can true sustainability, for example, be based on a foundation of nonrenewable natural resources such as fossil fuels? Not likely, and yet fossil fuels underlie virtually everything we do, the entirety of the way we live and the value system we live by. Can true sustainability be based on an energy-intensive, profligate, wasteful lifestyle such as the world has never seen? Not likely. Can true sustainability be based on a value system which, at best, concerns itself with miles per gallon in a vehicle but never questions how or for what purpose a vehicle is being used, who or what it is transporting, and why? Not with any application of honesty. Can true sustainability be related to a consumptive lifestyle that knows no limit (and refuses to consider any concept of limits), a lifestyle predicated on growth for its own sake (the disease of "growthism," which is what unrestrained capitalism is all about)? No, not if we are rational.

Sustainability, therefore, that is, any honest use of the word, requires far more than the cheap, shallow, superficial, and inherently dishonest measures in our behavior toward the planet which we commonly call examples of sustainability, whether in sustainable agriculture and food systems, sustainable usages of energy, and other ways we utilize or relate to creation. Sustainability, in fact, requires a change in our fundamental values. It requires us to be fundamentally countercultural and revolutionary, at least with regard to the common culture and its evolution since the Second World War, if not earlier.

A monk of my acquaintance in Minnesota once remarked to me that sustainability is a conversion experience. The secular world might scoff at this, figuring that a phrase like "conversion experience" might be what one would expect from a monk, a priest, a clergyman. And yet, when one thinks about it, is not such a "conversion experience" precisely what is called for if we are to meet the expectations even of our own rationality? Surely, a true change in our system of values, if that is indeed what is called for, could only occur as a conversion experience, for it would necessitate a fundamental change from deep within us. Not simply to alter how we do things but to change the value presupposition of why we do things is a conversion of the deepest kind.

If, therefore, we argue that sustainability of necessity is a conversion experience, if it is and must be predicated on a deep change of values themselves and not a half-hearted patch-it-up enterprise, then its expectation cannot be lodged in the prevailing value system, the dominant paradigm as it is called. It must come from a deeper place.

We might ask where we might find models of real sustainability. The location of such models should correlate to places, locations, people who put their faith in places other than within the dominant value system. They should be found among people who have developed a deep spirituality, a transcendent spirituality. They should be found among people who place their faith in something bigger than they are, in contrast to those who commonly place their faith in things smaller than they are (including, for example, the mall, shopping, consumption, the car, science, technology, the "techno-fix," economic growth, growthism, money, power, etc., any or all of which might readily become gods or idols in people's lives). In contrast, those who place their faith in things bigger than they are, things that transcend them, things that were there before them, things that will be there after them, things beyond their ability to encapsulate or comprehend, or know or delimit, whether one God, multiple gods, mystery, nature, the cosmos, etc., might demonstrate a greater ability to recognize, to demonstrate, to practice, to truly know sustainability.

Where might we have hope of finding such counter-cultural behavior, such sustainable behavior? One such place might be among people of faith. This does not necessarily mean "people of faith" in the narrow reduced way the world too often defines such people, that is, members of churches, baptized persons, persons who make claims about faith, though the phrase can include them. But rather it signifies people who are deeply spiritual (whether that spirituality shows itself or not), who do have faith in mystery, in something which is not them, and which transcends their being. A possible place for the evolution and maturation of true values of sustainability, therefore, might be in communities of such people, in "faith communities," but it would not likely be inclusive of all people in such communities, for such communities are part of the same corrupt unsustainable culture in which all of us, to a greater or lesser degree, live our lives.

Some such people might call themselves Christian. (If one follows Jesus Christ to the crucifixion, one might argue a lack of sustainability, but then there is the resurrection — a very different story.) No doubt Jesus Christ was a practitioner par excellence of countercultural behavior, of radicalism, of revolution. And capital punishment was a natural response by the society of his day. That society knew an enemy, a troublemaker of serious proportions, when it saw one, and acted accordingly (albeit while running the risk of creating a martyr, which it did and which has been done since). So sustainability might be found within or among some groups of Christians, for Christians claim to believe in a transcendent God, and also believe in immanence, of the Creator in the created, of God in all, and therefore, ideally, of the sacrality of all things. They believe in the Great Chain of Being, as Richard Rohr has remarked.

Monastics of all stripes, Christian, Hindu, Buddhist, are by definition (and to their ideal) also countercultural. For the Christian-related reasons already alluded to, and for other reasons, one might hope to find some true sustainability among them. However, in addition to being human, they are not totally removed from our culture or the times in which we all live, so they might not always yield good models. But the potential is there.

Indigenous peoples, with their earth-centered reverence for creation, for the sacrality of all, with creation-oriented traditions evolving over many centuries, might also be a place to seek models of sustainability, models which are spiritually based. In addition to being part of the anti-sustainable, anti-ecological corruptions of our own times and our own world, however, indigenous peoples often have an additional heavy burden, the yoke of many generations of oppression and of destruction of their culture, which leaves so many of them incapable of carrying leadership responsibility. They are just too weighted down. But since they are countercultural, we should not ignore them as models.

There are undoubtedly other places to look for true models of sustainability. Our own ability to contemplate and reflect will undoubtedly help us to find more such models and to help others do likewise. Let us not, however, underestimate the task at hand. Let us not be tempted to accept false models as we so readily fall into the trap of adoring false idols. Let us strive to understand that sustainability is indeed a conversion experience. Faith, prayer, contemplation, and action are all necessary elements in our finding, learning from, and putting into practice real sustainability. Let us persevere until we find the truth.

21

Freeing the Soul through Art

BARBARA COLEMAN

 Great art has a curious life of its own. I read a marvelous story once, based on the documentary *From Mao to Mozart,* about a visit to China made by the conductor and violinist Isaac Stern. At the time of his visit, Chinese musicians had been forbidden to listen to or to play Western music for many years. They had requested Stern's help in interpreting Western music. A Chinese orchestra played a Mozart composition with masterful technical skill and energy. While well played, the composition came across as rather mechanical and lifeless. It was not music yet because the orchestra members did not *feel* it or really *hear* it. They could not create music until they could hear it inwardly and intuitively.

Music is not created just by people playing musical instruments, but by music playing through people — playing through the individual consciousness of each musician. The individual consciousness becomes the true instrument.

Isaac Stern listened closely to the musicians, some of whom were extremely self-conscious about rehearsing for him. At times, Stern would replay sections of the score, thus enabling them to have a first-hand experience of the music. The Chinese played the notes correctly but Stern made the music come alive. Having thus experienced the difference, the musicians were able to let the music itself direct all of their professional skill in such a way as to let music happen.

Great art, like great music, needs technical expertise as well as unchecked creativity, passion, and expression. Great art seems to be created through a person. Somehow one's ego, self-consciousness, and expectations must be released before the piece is completed. The visual arts are full of examples of compositions being imbued with a life of their own, similar to the musical composition just described. A portrait by Rembrandt and a vase of sunflowers painted by Van Gogh burst with vitality and passion. Art is so subtle, so spiritual, that only a direct experience with it can guide the painter to animate blobs of paint into something that can live and breathe on its own.

Many of the young children I have taught in the elementary schools recognize and respond joyfully to the art experience. They unself-consciously dive in and become consumed with their feelings, their sensations, the tactile expression of the paint and are rarely, if ever, concerned with proper technique. They create lively and genuinely unique works of art. Frustration occurs, yes, but it is the frustration akin to a child's learning how to walk. Each fall is not taken as a personal failure to a child highly motivated to walk: it is rather that the child is experimenting and learning the physical laws of nature. A child expressing himself artistically is experiencing the great freedom of learning that is guided by art itself.

Why is it that some children cannot joyfully dive in? There are a myriad of reasons, I'm sure, but the most common one I've seen, in children and adults alike, is that they have become limited by being self-conscious of their ability. This self-consciousness begins early in life and seems to come about when either praise or criticism gets too personal. An example from my own life might best illustrate what I mean by becoming "too personal."

When my oldest daughter was three, she would sit and paint for long periods of time in my studio as I painted. I was thrilled with her work (and thrilled that she could sit for so long a time!), and I told her so. I praised her extravagantly, hoping to encourage her. I would say, "Oh, you really are a great artist!" and things of that sort. As soon as I would begin this personal praise, her interest in her work would wane and within minutes her work would become sloppy or careless or she'd just get up and leave. Clearly my praise was having an unintended and very undesirable effect on her. I was making her self-conscious and distracting her from her discoveries. She began to turn to me for praise and approval, and the possibility of self-doubt was introduced ("Would Mommy like this one?"). It didn't take long to redirect her focus back to her work, once I stopped praising her and addressed my comments to what was on the page. Understanding and discovery are their own rewards. Her receptivity to art was a result of her lack of self-consciousness, and this allowed her to see what is and thus draw and paint it.

When I am painting in the studio, there are a lot of people in there with me. I refer to them as "studio ghosts." Their presence is as real as if they were physically standing there. They include my teachers, critics, friends, husband, gallery owners, my favorite artists in history...and one by one, if I'm really painting, they walk out. If I am *really* painting, *I* walk out too. Those paintings are invariably the best and I am so grateful for the experience of painting and for the changes in my seeing, that the painting itself is pure gift. Then the noun "painting" becomes inseparable from the verb or action of "painting." Being unself-conscious and being willing to lose oneself in the work is vital for a child and an artist.

So how can we respond to a child's artwork? With genuine appreciation and enthusiasm, I think, such as "What marvelous colors you chose," or "Tell me about your painting." A child can also become self-conscious if her view of the world is invalidated, such as "*That* doesn't look like a tree." There is no way that art can reach and guide a child if he is too locked up to enjoy himself. How can we free him up to learn and have the experience of creating art? As a parent and art teacher, I find that the more that the child and I can focus on the immediate artwork at hand, the more satisfying the experience becomes. By not emphasizing a product, and by focusing on process instead, the work becomes more successful as well. The more that the child is able to reach a state of awareness in which her self-consciousness disappears into the desire to participate and see what she is trying to express, the more the art can reach her. I am inspired by the story of Isaac Stern and the Chinese musicians. As a conductor, *all* (!) he had to do was to hear, feel, and lose himself in the music, and thereby open opportunities for others to experience and create it as well.

22

Blue Dresses in the Jungle

AVIS CROWE

 Tears streamed down my cheeks as I drove along the highway, moved to the depths as my husband read aloud from an old book of my mother's. The slender volume was Norman Cousins's account of his visit in the 1950s to Albert Schweitzer at Lambarene, the remarkable hospital he had carved out of the African jungle. The tears were a surprise. I had read the book years ago and much had happened in my life in the intervening time. Now I listened with very different ears. What caught me off guard was the description of a routine day that was transformed by an ordinary blue cotton dress.

Life in the jungle compound was harsh, demanding, and basic. The doctor was kind and benevolent but could also be stern and by his own example demanded 150 percent of everyone on the staff. They gave it willingly. Each person there had been drawn to this lonely outpost not only to work beside the legendary doctor but for precisely the opportunity to be fully engaged in work that was necessary and satisfying. They had given up a great deal to be part of Schweitzer's team. None, apparently, saw it as a sacrifice. The days were long, the needs endless. They waged war not only against illness and ignorance but against the jungle itself. There was little time or thought left for recreation and pure pleasure. By the end of the day and a simple meal eaten together in the communal dining room, the staff usually dispersed to their own quarters for a bit of reading or attention to personal tasks before falling exhausted into bed.

But this day would be different. Clara Urguhart, a friend of Dr. Schweitzer who had visited Lambarene before and was an accomplished photographer, had come with Cousins on this trip to document the visit. She had brought surprise gifts for the women on the staff, a bright-colored cotton dress for each of them. There were squeals of pleasure when the nurses opened their gifts and held them up for each other to see and admire. They called Dr. Margaret, known to all as "La Doctoresse" and a favorite of everyone, to claim her dress: She graciously accepted a long blue cotton dress from Clara and rushed off to try it on. When she returned, the nurse in charge of the lepers exclaimed breathlessly that La Doctoresse looked like a movie star. The nurses then disappeared to try on their new frocks and returned moving like models on a runway. Cousins writes, "It almost seemed as though the place had been touched with magic." They danced up and down the porch, dresses "swooshing and swirling," admiring one another and themselves, faces filled with delight and wonder at this unexpected bounty.

The most reserved of the nurses suddenly clapped her hands like a child and said, "Tonight we will have a party. We will surprise Dr. Schweitzer. We will wear our dresses to dinner. And we will fix our hair." The enthusiasm was contagious, and these jungle doctors and nurses suddenly were like schoolgirls preparing for the prom. Intelligent, serious, highly trained women, they were not given to vanity. They paid scant attention to their appearance. But Clara knew that they were still women who needed the chance now and then to be feminine, even in the middle of a jungle compound. She had known intuitively just what would bring out the neglected, softer side of these dedicated workers.

When Dr. Schweitzer came into the dining room that evening, he was greeted by candlelight and women adorned in brightly colored dresses. Some had ribbons in their hair and were even wearing lipstick. Norman Cousins described the doctor's reaction:

> His eyes danced behind the craglike brows. I could see he had a vast delight. "Thank you for letting me come to your banquet," he said in the manner of a man who had just arrived at the Queen's ball. Then when he sat down and customary silence occurred so that he could say grace, he said he had forgotten all the grace prayers he ever knew.

The other male staff were obviously pleased, and everyone's delight rose another notch when the doctor declared he also had something to share: real butter and a bottle of fine wine that had been a gift and was being saved for a special occasion. Dinner times at the compound were usually routine, with conversation focused on patients, medical matters, how to deal with the latest incursions of the jungle. But on this night they were all special guests at a fine banquet, and talk turned to more carefree and frivolous subjects, including a sparkling mini-monologue by the learned doctor about how champagne is made. A special glow lit up the dining room; it was not only from candles.

They ended the meal with the customary hymn singing and Dr. Schweitzer reading the Lord's Prayer in German. The mood was relaxed and expansive. After Schweitzer had adjourned to his room, the others stayed on chatting quietly, reluctant to break the spell. A deep sense of gratitude and peace had taken hold of everyone and spilled over to fill the entire compound.

And I, driving along a Texas highway at year's end, 1994, wept. I thought about all the clothes hanging in my closet, the things that fill my life, the options that surround me. In the midst of such abundance it is so easy to lose the gratitude and wonder of a single new thing, so easy to overlook the gifts that are all around me; so easy to acquire more — another book, another improvement for the house, another turtleneck because I "need" another color. I wept for the beauty of those women: their purpose and dedication, the simplicity of a life without the clutter of our middle-class "too-muchness." I wept because of the transforming power of a simple blue cotton dress and because the people of Lambarene understood that power and were able to receive it with childlike wholeheartedness, as a gift of grace to be honored and celebrated by the entire community.

23

Simplicity as a Key to Holiness of Life

WAYNE TEASDALE

We live in a culture with which we continuously make our compromises. There is so much to admire about American society, for instance, the opportunities and resources to pursue our interests or our unique spiritual path. Even though we may criticize the American way of life in our countercultural moments, particularly when we view it through the clear lens of our faith and the uncompromising vision of the Gospel, we all love our common culture in some way. I find this is especially true of myself.

Keeping the above in mind, let me offer an insight into the nature of simplicity that is not meant to denigrate our culture, but to suggest a spiritual resource to deepen our understanding of what God requires of us as he invites us into greater intimacy with him. The Gospel is essentially an ethics of love and a guide to relationship with him, with nature, with others, and with our own true selves. Relationship with the Divine, which is the real purpose of all prayer, is deep, abiding friendship with him; it is to reach and dwell in a powerfully transforming communion with the Persons of the Trinity. We are made for friendship with the Divine, and we need to be who we really are in order to cultivate this depth of friendship with God. Our true selves have a lot to do with how we have been wrought by the Creator, that is, made in the image and likeness of God. Simplicity uncovers for us the existential depth and reality of being an image and likeness of God, while our culture would lull us into an abysmal distraction and the pettiness of the consumer mentality.

Again, there is so much that is good in our culture, but there is equally a lot that is detrimental to following the Gospel. To put the matter as simply as I can, it can be observed that American society is spiritually illiterate, morally confused, psychologically dysfunctional, and addicted to violence, consumerism, and endless amounts of entertainment. Indeed, we live from movie to movie. As I write this we are in a transition between *Harry Potter* and *The Lord of the Rings,* which will open on December 19. Our culture is also in love with violence; it is a culture of violence, which it maintains with Hollywood's willful and gleeful complicity.

Simplicity itself alerts us to the truth so eloquently emphasized by Jesus that we should "not store up our treasures on earth where moth and thief can get at them." Simplicity is not about *having* more, but *being* more. Being more is related to developing an attitude of loving-kindness, of compassionate action, mercy, kindness, and sensitivity. These are divine qualities. Sensitivity is a vast awareness; it requires that we make room for others, especially God, within ourselves. We must achieve our innate spaciousness. Vast sensitivity is a spacious being; it approximates the divine being. The Divine is infinite spaciousness totally animated by love. Christ enfleshed the spaciousness of God's Love for us in the event of the Incarnation, an existential teaching for humankind and beyond.

We cannot discover and cultivate our own innate vastness, our spaciousness as images and likenesses of the divine glory, if we are interiorly obsessed with the twin culture of entertainment and consumerism that surrounds us here in America. We have to liberate ourselves from this self-imposed complexity that so clutters our souls and oppresses our consciences in relation to the have-nots, the two-thirds of humanity living in conditions of nearly perpetual destitution. Simplicity becomes for us all a vehicle through the clutter, the possessive quality of our society, the relentless drive to have the impermanent. We must free ourselves, through a voluntarily simple life, from the radical attachment to the impermanent.

If we are to awaken more deeply to the divine sensitivity that is our nature as reflections of the glory that God quite simply is, we must remove the obstacles in ourselves to this high estate of being. It is simplicity of life that guides us in this kind of growth by removing the obstructions our culture has taught us. These are obstacles that stem from our own incapacity for generosity, our uncritical individualism, our selfishness, and they need to be set aside in acts of generosity, love, and profound kindness. Simplicity is our teacher in healing and expanding our relationship with God, with others, with the natural world, and with ourselves.

Simplicity of life directs us to take only what we require for our lives and leave the rest for the sake of the larger community and the desperate need of the marginalized poor. It is the constant realization that only God matters, and is the absolute task of charity, of loving others in a nonsentimental cherishing of the members of the Mystical Body. In a very real sense, one lesson of September 11 is a curiously Gospel insight: the temporary state of earthly happiness and the necessity of giving our attention and commitment to the kingdom of heaven. It teaches us further how unjust our possessiveness is, our lack of simplicity, when it results in the diminishment of most of humankind. To live in this way blocks us from the realization of our own personal responsibility in the terrible plight of the poor and the oppressed around the world. Until all have sufficient food, clothing, shelter, education, and medical care, there is no real justice in the world and, thus, no grounds for a permanent global peace.

Francis of Assisi, Mother Teresa, Charles de Foucauld, and countless others are prophets of holy poverty, of that vital attitude and spiritual practice of simplicity of life that actually clarifies everything for us. They understood so well how necessary this practical virtue is for our relationship with nature, with God, and with the poor who surround us, as well as for our spiritual lives if they are to be authentic.

It is only through simplicity that our relationship with the Divine is single-minded and pure; it is focused, and our hearts then are undivided and free of preoccupation with the lesser goods of this world. With this kind of commitment to a voluntary sense of Gospel poverty, our relationship with God can soar to the heights of union, communion, and effective acts of mercy. Simplicity of life establishes a new relationship with the natural world; it makes true harmony possible, and in this harmony Francis of Assisi is again our teacher. The simple life is one in connection with nature, in awe of her beauty, and aware of our essential dependence on her. Living simply each day of our lives allows us to be genuinely part of nature, which is the real first world. It makes it possible, furthermore, to be one with the poor because we are also poor. To be poor, in the sense in which Jesus advocates, allows us to be truly available to others, because, like them, we are vulnerable. Finally, simplicity, poverty of spirit, frees us in our own spiritual journey and teaches us in the flesh, so to speak, the radical freedom of a nonpossessive attitude toward life, what the Gospel, in the example and words of Jesus, manifests as indispensable to us in our own journey to God here in this world. Simplicity of life leads to genuine selfless love, summed up so eloquently by the poet Allen Ginsberg: "Holy is the supernatural extra brilliant kindness of the soul."

About Richard Rohr

Richard Rohr, O.F.M., is a Franciscan priest of the New Mexico Province. He was the founder of the New Jerusalem Community in Cincinnati, Ohio, in 1971, and, in 1986, the Center for Action and Contemplation in Albuquerque, New Mexico, where he presently serves as Founding Director. The Center is intended to serve a dual purpose, not only as a radical voice for peaceful, nonviolent social change but also as a forum for renewal and encouragement for the individual who seeks direction from and understanding of God's will and love.

Richard was born in 1943 in Kansas. He entered the Franciscans in 1961 and was ordained to the priesthood in 1970. He received his master's degree in theology from Dayton that same year. He now lives in a hermitage behind his Franciscan community in Albuquerque and divides his time between local work and preaching and teaching on all continents. He is well known for his numerous audio and videotapes and for his articles in the Center's newsletter, *Radical Grace*. He is a regular contributing editor/writer for *Sojourners* magazine and recently published a seven-part Lenten series for the *National Catholic Reporter*. He has a best-selling tape series called *The NEW Great Themes of Scripture*. Fr. Rohr has authored books in the areas of male spirituality, the use of the Enneagram in spiritual direction, Scripture, spirituality, and contemplative prayer.

For more information about the Center for Contemplation and Action in Albuquerque, New Mexico, please look on the web at *www.cacradicalgrace.org*.

crossroad

Also by Richard Rohr

ADAM'S RETURN
The Five Promises of Male Initiation

Best-selling author Richard Rohr, a leader in the renaissance in male spirituality, offers the fruit of his travel and experience to explain the importance of male initiation and male elders in healthy psychological and spiritual life.

EVERYTHING BELONGS
The Gift of Contemplative Prayer

"Rohr at his finest: insightful cultural critique — with strong connection to the marginalized." *— The Other Side*

A personal retreat for those who hunger for a deeper prayer life but don't know what contemplation really is or how to let it happen.

Check your local bookstore for availability.
To order directly from the publisher,
please call 1-800-888-4741 for Customer Service
or visit our Web site at *www.cpcbooks.com.*
For catalog orders, please send your request to the address below.

info@CrossroadPublishing.com
THE CROSSROAD PUBLISHING COMPANY

All prices subject to change.

crossroad